Global Positioning Systems

Global Positioning Systems

By Laurie Collier Hillstrom

LUCENT BOOKS
A part of Gale, Cengage Learning

GALE
CENGAGE Learning™

Detroit • New York • San Francisco • New Haven, Conn • Waterville, Maine • London

LIBRARY OF CONGRESS CATALOGING-IN-PUBLICATION DATA

Hillstrom, Laurie Collier, 1965-
    Global positioning systems / by Laurie Collier Hillstrom.
        p. cm.--(Technology 360)
    Includes bibliographical references and index.
    ISBN 978-1-4205-0325-8 (hardcover)
    1. **Global Positioning System.** I. Title.
    G109.5.H54 2010
    910.285—dc22

                                                        2010030623

Lucent Books
27500 Drake Rd
Farmington Hills MI 48331

ISBN-13: 978-1-4205-0325-8
ISBN-10: 1-4205-0325-1

Printed in the United States of America
 2 3 4 5 6 7 14 13 12 11 10

CONTENTS

"As we go forward, I hope we're going to continue to use technology to make really big differences in how people live and work."
—Sergey Brin, co-founder of Google

The past few decades have seen some amazing advances in technology. Many of these changes have had a direct and measureable impact on the way people live, work, and play. Communication tools, such as cell phones, satellites, and the Internet, allow people to keep in constant contact across longer distances and from the most remote places. In fields related to medicine, existing technologies—digital imaging devices, robotics, and lasers, for example—are being used to redefine surgical procedures and diagnostic techniques. As technology has become more complex, however, so have the related ethical, legal, and safety issues.

Psychologist B.F. Skinner once noted that "the real problem is not whether machines think but whether men do." Recent advances in technology have, in many cases, drastically changed the way people view the world around them. They can have a conversation with someone across the globe at lightning speed, access a huge universe of information with the click of a key, or become an avatar in a virtual world of their own making. While advances like these have been viewed as a great boon in some quarters, they have also opened the door to questions about whether or not the speed of technological advancement has come at an unspoken price. A closer examination of the evolution and use of these devices provides a deeper understanding of the social, cultural and ethical implications that they may hold for our future.

Technology 360 not only explores how evolving technologies work, but also examines the short- and long-term impact of their use on society as a whole. Each volume in Technology 360 focuses on a particular invention, device or family of similar devices, exploring how the device was developed; how it works; its impact on society; and possible future uses. Volumes also contain a timeline specific to each topic, a glossary of technical terms used in the text, and a subject index. Sidebars, photos and detailed illustrations, tables, charts and graphs help further illuminate the text.

Titles in this series emphasize inventions and devices familiar to most readers, such as robotics, digital cameras, iPods, and video games. Not only will users get an easy-to-understand, "nuts and bolts" overview of these inventions, they will also learn just how much these devices have evolved. For example, in 1973 a Motorola cell phone weighed about 2 pounds (.907kg) and cost $4000.00—today, cell phones weigh only a few ounces and are inexpensive enough for every member of the family to have one. Lasers—long a staple of the industrial world—have become highly effective surgical tools, capable of reshaping the cornea of the eye and cleaning clogged arteries. Early video games were played on large machines in arcades; now, many families play games on sophisticated home systems that allow for multiple players and cross-location networking.

IMPORTANT DATES

1759
British clock maker John Harrison revolutionizes ocean navigation by inventing the marine chronometer.

1957
The Soviet Union launches the first manmade satellite into orbit.

1973
The U.S. Department of Defense approves the Navigation Signal Timing and Ranging (NAVSTAR) program for Global Positioning System development.

1907
Italian engineers Ettore Bellini and Alessandro Tosi create the first radio direction finder.

1900   **1935**   **1970**

1940s
The U.S. Coast Guard develops the Long Range Navigation (LORAN) system.

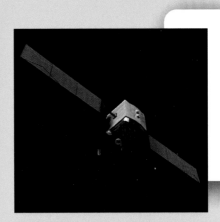

1978
The first NAVSTAR Block I satellite is launched.

1983

President Ronald Reagan declassifies the NAVSTAR program, making the Global Positioning System available for civilian use.

1991

The U.S. military demonstrates the usefulness of Global Positioning System technology during the Persian Gulf War.

2014

Next-generation Block III Global Positioning System satellites are scheduled for launch.

1990　　　　　　**2010**　　　　　　**2030**

1995

The full constellation of twenty-four Global Positioning System navigational satellites is declared operational.

2000

President Bill Clinton announces that the U.S. military will stop intentionally degrading the quality of the Global Positioning System satellite signal (Selective Availability); Global Positioning System enthusiast Dave Ulmer creates geocaching, a treasure-hunt game.

A Revolution in Navigation

The Global Positioning System (GPS) consists of satellites in Earth's orbit that transmit radio signals back to Earth and receiver units on Earth that use these signals to calculate their exact geographic location. As recently as the 1980s, most Americans would have dismissed the idea of a satellite-based navigation system as pure science fiction. Back then, it was a cumbersome process for people to determine their precise position in latitude and longitude or to figure out the best route to follow to reach a desired location. Travelers had to consult paper maps and guidebooks, measure distances, use a compass, watch carefully for signs and landmarks, and sometimes even stop to ask local residents for directions. People needed skills, knowledge, and common sense to reach their desired destination.

Today hundreds of millions of people around the world take GPS technology for granted because it has become such a fixture in modern life. Satellite navigation information is available everywhere, twenty-four hours a day, in all kinds of weather conditions, and free of charge. GPS has revolutionized navigation and fundamentally transformed the way individuals and businesses go about their daily activities. People can easily view satellite maps online, get detailed directions to virtually any destination, plot routes through the wilderness, or simply stand in the middle of nowhere and still know exactly where they are. "The system provides a novel, unique, and instantly available address for every square yard on the surface of the planet—a new international standard for locations and distances," according to scientist Daniel Kleppner and science journalist Gary Taubes, writing for the National Academy of Sciences. "To the computers of the world, at least, our locations may be defined not by a street address, a city, and a state, but by a longitude and a latitude."[1]

Despite its relatively short history, GPS technology has already found a huge variety of applications. It is used to guide military weapons, survey property boundaries and construction sites, conduct scientific research, coordinate emergency response efforts, enhance outdoor recreational activities, and help automobiles, ships, and planes navigate safely. Although it is difficult to measure the full impact of GPS, it is clear that the technology has become an indispensable part of modern life. In a 2009 *GPS World* magazine article, authors Stephen T. Powers and Brad Parkinson write, "Over the past 30 years, [GPS] has steadily and stealthily crept into the fabric of worldwide society, creating capabilities and dependencies that did not exist before.... With more than a billion GPS receivers in use, this stunning achievement has truly revolutionized the way the world functions in the 21st century."[2]

CHAPTER **1**

A Brief History of Navigation Systems

T hroughout human history, people have traveled in search of food, water, and other necessities of life. Over time people have developed increasingly sophisticated tools and methods to aid them in navigation. The earliest travelers navigated by sight. They memorized the natural features of the land around them and used this knowledge to find their way back to desirable locations. They also passed down territorial details and navigational information from one generation to the next. Once settlements and cities formed, residents erected signs, identified prominent landscape features, and built monuments to serve as landmarks for travelers. But sight navigation had some disadvantages. It was dependent on good visibility, for instance, and landmarks—whether natural or manmade— often changed or disappeared over time.

With the development of written language, people began recording navigational information on maps. The earliest known maps were created more than four thousand years ago in ancient Egypt and Babylonia (a kingdom in the southern part of modern-day Iraq). Engraved on stone or clay tablets, these maps tended to focus on practical information, like property boundaries and relationships between objects, rather than visual representations of the known world. Maps grew increasingly sophisticated over time as the science of geography developed, incorporating elements of mathematics, astronomy, and engineering.

An important element of geography appeared around 300 B.C., when Greek philosophers began using latitude and longitude to designate locations on maps. Once they realized that the earth was shaped like a sphere, they knew that the distance around the planet could be divided into 360 degrees. They drew lines on maps to create a grid that divided the earth into sections or quadrants.

Latitude and Longitude

The grid system developed by the Greeks starts with an imaginary, horizontal line around the middle of the planet called the equator, which is designated as 0 degrees. Latitude measures the distance in degrees north or south of the equator. The North Pole has a latitude of 90 degrees north, while the South Pole has a latitude of 90 degrees south. Every other location on Earth has a latitude between 0 and 90 degrees north or between 0 and 90 degrees south of the equator. Lines of latitude, known as parallels, run parallel to the equator and are evenly spaced approximately 69 miles (111km) apart.

Longitude measures the distance around Earth from an imaginary, vertical line called the prime meridian, which runs from the North Pole to the South Pole through Greenwich, England, and the Atlantic Ocean. The prime meridian has a longitude of 0 degrees. The imaginary line at 180 degrees longitude, directly opposite the prime meridian in the middle of the Pacific Ocean, is called the international date line. Every other location on the planet has a longitude between 0 and 180 degrees east or between 0 and 180 degrees west of the prime meridian.

Lines of longitude, known as meridians, run perpendicular to the equator. The distance between them varies from

The earliest maps, such as this one of Xian, China, were carved on stone. They recorded practical information, including property boundaries.

Latitude and longitude lines are important markers for determining time as well as location. Time zones are divided every 15 degrees longitude, so that the sun is at its highest at noon for every location, as Earth rotates. GPS satellites run on the Universal Standard Time, or the time recorded along the Prime Meridian. Individual GPS receivers must use software to adjust this time to reflect their time zones.

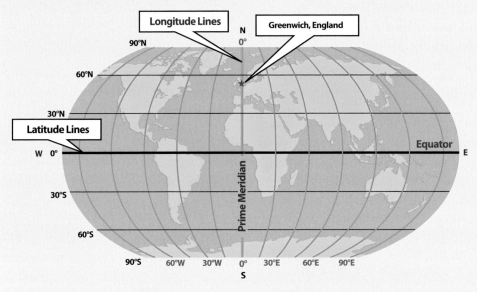

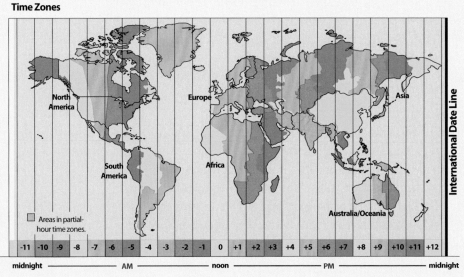

Time Zones

approximately 69 miles (111km) at the equator to 0 when the lines converge at the poles. Each degree of latitude or longitude can be divided into sixty minutes, and each minute can be further divided into sixty seconds. A minute of latitude is approximately 1.2 miles (1.9km); a second of latitude is approximately 100 feet (30m). Minutes and seconds of longitude vary due to the variations in longitude size. The latitude and longitude of Washington, D.C., for example, are 38 degrees, 53 minutes, and 42 seconds north latitude (abbreviated 38°53'42"N) and 77 degrees, 2 minutes, and 12 seconds west longitude (abbreviated 77°02'12"W).

Navigation on Water

Sight navigation and land maps had limited usefulness for early explorers on the open ocean, where there were no landmarks and reference points to guide them. Nevertheless, many ancient peoples built boats and went to sea, beginning

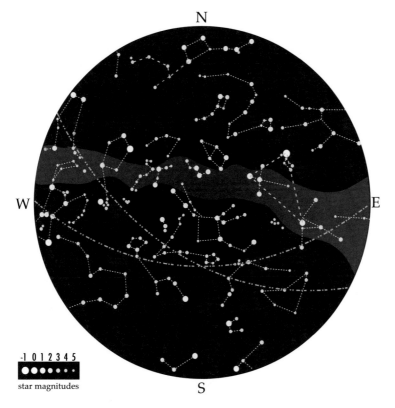

star magnitudes

Early sailors used constellations to guide them in their navigation of the seas.

The marine chronometer, like this one from the Titanic, allowed sailors to determine their longitude against a fixed position.

with the Phoenicians around 2000 B.C. Most early mariners stayed within sight of land and followed coastal landmarks. They grew bolder over time as they learned more about prevailing currents, seasonal wind patterns, and the habits of marine life and sea birds.

Persians, Arabs, Pacific Islanders, and other early sailors ventured farther out into the open sea by using landmarks in the sky for navigation. They memorized the nighttime sky and created celestial maps showing the position of various stars in different seasons. The Vikings sailed across the northern Atlantic Ocean to reach North America in A.D. 1000 by observing wind and wave patterns, as well as the sun, moon, and stars.

By the middle of the fifteenth century, the science of astronomy had developed to the point where it provided a fairly reliable means of water navigation. Portuguese sailors relied on celestial navigation in exploring the southern coast of Africa and thousands of miles of open ocean in the 1400s. As people gained knowledge and experience with sea navigation, they kept records and made maps of their voyages. Over time they also developed increasingly accurate instruments to help them navigate the open ocean and to calculate their direction and position.

Early Navigation Tools

The mid-1400s saw an explosion in ocean exploration thanks to improvements in navigation tools. Many mariners of this period carried a device called a quadrant to determine their approximate latitude. A quadrant consisted of a quarter circle made of wood or brass with 90 degrees marked along the curved edge. A weighted string called a plumb line hung down from the point. Sailors could line up the quadrant with a celestial body, read the angle to the horizon indicated by the plumb line, and compare the reading to a star chart to figure out their latitude. The accuracy of quadrants was limited, however, and the instruments were difficult to use in rough seas.

Another navigation aid that proved helpful to fifteenth-century sailors was the astrolabe. This circular device, resembling a wheel or a plate, was usually engraved with pictures showing the positions of major constellations (star formations). By measuring the angle of the sun overhead at its highest point and observing the constellations visible at sunrise and sunset, mariners were able to calculate their approximate latitude. Although the astrolabe was easier to use than the quadrant, it still required some skill to measure angles on a rocking ship at sea.

The introduction of the sextant in the 1700s helped solve the problem of taking celestial measurements on the unsteady deck of a ship. The sextant was designed around 1730 by two inventors working independently, Englishman John Hadley (1682–1744) and American Thomas Godfrey (1704–1749). This instrument used double reflecting mirrors to make it easier to measure the angle of the sun, moon, or stars above the horizon. Of course, the device still required sailors to look at the sky, so it could not be used during storms or heavy cloud cover. Nevertheless, sextants provided such a good approximation of latitude that some modern ships keep one onboard as a backup in case the electronic instruments fail.

Another navigational tool that has retained its usefulness in the modern world is the compass. A compass is basically a magnetized needle that aligns with the earth's magnetic field to point north. Chinese sailors began using it as a navigational aid around A.D. 1100, and its use quickly spread to other regions of the world. The problem with early compasses, however, was that they tended to be unreliable. The needles could be attracted by iron objects, react to magnetic storms like the northern lights, or lose their magnetism for unexplained reasons. The development of steel needles in the mid-1700s improved the reliability of compasses, allowing navigators to follow a course bearing measured in degrees away from true north.

Longitude and the Chronometer

Under ideal conditions, early ocean explorers used a combination of navigational tools, like the compass, astrolabe, sextant, and quadrant, to determine their direction of travel and estimate their latitude (north-south position) to within a few miles. Until the late eighteenth century, however, sailors could not get an exact fix on their longitude (east-west position). Since the earth is constantly rotating, calculating longitude required sailors to keep track of time. For every 15 degrees of longitude that they traveled, the local time changed by one hour. Although sailors could figure out the time at their current location by measuring the position of the sun, they also needed to know the time at a fixed reference point in order to calculate their longitude. Accurate time measurement made it easy to find longitude. If the angle of the sun told ship's navigators that it was noon in their current location, for instance, and an onboard clock said that it was midnight in London, England, the navigators could determine that they were exactly halfway around the world from London. But no clocks existed that could keep time accurately at sea until the late 1700s.

This difficulty led to some historic mistakes in navigation. Explorer Christopher Columbus, for example, made his famous 1492 journey west across the Atlantic Ocean with a crew of cartographers equipped with quadrants and

Radio Signals

All types of wireless communication, including GPS satellite signals, depend on radio waves. Radio waves are composed of electrical and magnetic energy that travels through space. These electromagnetic waves vary in terms of their amplitude (the strength or height of each wave) and frequency (how often the wave pattern repeats itself). Radio waves occur in a continuous spectrum of different frequencies, sort of like the colors of the rainbow in the spectrum of visible light.

GPS satellite data or other communication signals are attached to radio waves through a process called modulation. Modulating a radio wave involves changing one or both of its basic characteristics. In amplitude modulation (AM) the strength or height of the wave changes. Changing the repetition pattern of the wave is called frequency modulation (FM). All other types of modulation are variations or combinations of AM and FM. Since the radio spectrum is limited, the Federal Communications Commission assigns frequencies for different uses through a system of licenses.

compasses. But when he landed on an island in the Caribbean (around 75 degrees west longitude), he thought he had reached India (around 75 degrees east longitude)—on the opposite side of the world. Columbus and other mariners of his era had only rudimentary methods of keeping track of time onboard their ships. Many sailors used sand-filled hour glasses that had to be watched carefully and turned over regularly. Over a long voyage, small errors in timekeeping had a cumulative effect. A loss of even ten minutes per day could cause a computational error of 150 miles (241km) or more.

Fixing a position at sea became much easier after 1759, when British clock maker John Harrison (1693–1776) invented the marine chronometer. This device informed mariners around the world of the current time in Greenwich, England, giving sailors a fixed reference point with which to determine longitude. It was accurate to within a few seconds, even after weeks at sea. It was unaffected by motion, temperature changes, or high humidity. The marine chronometer soon proved to be a tremendous advance to navigation. Captain James Cook (1728–1779), a British naval officer, used it to sail all the way around the world in 1779. Cook's calculations of longitude proved correct to within 8 miles (13km) throughout his voyage. The ability to determine his position allowed Cook to create detailed maps of previously unexplored regions that provided valuable guidance to future travelers.

Radio Navigation

The next major advance in navigation technology took place in the early twentieth century, when the directional radio antenna was developed. Radio waves are a form of electromagnetic energy that travel through the air. German physicist Heinrich Hertz (1857–1894) first proved the existence of radio waves in a laboratory setting in 1887. Over the next two decades, inventors came up with a variety of devices to transmit and receive radio signals. They discovered that radio waves could travel over long distances and be used to carry messages and other information.

Scientists and engineers soon began investigating the possibility of using radio signals for navigation. In 1907 Italian engineers Ettore Bellini and Alessandro Tosi created the first useable radio direction finder (RDF). This device was basically an antenna for receiving radio signals, but it was able to pinpoint the direction from which a specific radio signal originated. Since the antenna broadcasting the signal was in a known, fixed location, determining the direction to the source provided an aid to navigation. An RDF offered a number of advantages over older celestial navigation methods. It could be used at any time of day, for instance, and it remained useful in bad weather. Before long, the U.S. government established networks of low-power radio beacons to provide navigational information, and increasing numbers of boats and planes were equipped with RDF antennas.

The development of radio detection and ranging (RADAR) technology in the 1930s enabled scientists to use radio

BITS & BYTES

7,000 miles per hour

Speed at which a GPS satellite orbits Earth.

waves to determine the location and direction of distant objects. Radar systems transmitted radio waves in a certain frequency and used a large, dish-shaped antenna to detect the waves as they bounced back. The pattern of the returning waves indicated the presence of objects beyond the range of vision. This proved helpful to navigation in the air and at sea during periods of low visibility. Pilots and captains could use radar to detect objects in their path and change course to avoid collisions.

During World War II, Allied military experts developed pulse radar. Pulse radar sent out radio signals in short, powerful bursts and measured the time it took for the signals to bounce back. Since system operators knew how fast the signals traveled, they could determine the exact location of enemy ships and planes.

The ability to measure minuscule time differences between the transmission and reception of radio signals found important civilian uses beginning in the 1940s, when the U.S. Coast Guard developed a radio navigation system called Long Range Navigation (LORAN). This system consisted of a network of

The development of RADAR in the 1930s bounced radio waves off of distant objects to determine their location.

radio towers—mostly located in coastal areas—that emitted pulsed radio signals. Ships and planes could use special equipment to receive the signal from various towers. By measuring the time between transmission and reception for signals from towers in known locations, captains and pilots could determine their current position in both latitude and longitude. LORAN proved to be a valuable navigation tool, with an accuracy of within 65 feet (20m). By the end of the twentieth century, however, this ground-based system had largely been replaced by the Global Positioning System (GPS), a new, space-based technology.

The Development of GPS

Although GPS operates on the same principles as LORAN and other radio navigation technologies, with GPS the transmission of radio signals originates on satellites orbiting

Ivan A. Getting

One of the people most responsible for the development of GPS navigation technology is Ivan A. Getting. He was born on January 18, 1912, in New York City. After studying physics at the Massachusetts Institute of Technology and astrophysics at Oxford University, he developed radar systems for the U.S. Army during World War II. He helped invent an automated microwave tracking system that enabled Allied antiaircraft guns to shoot down 95 percent of German V-1 bombs that targeted London during the war.

During the 1950s, Getting led the research and engineering division of the Raytheon Corporation. In this role, he promoted the concept of using satellite-based systems to calculate highly accurate positioning data for airplanes, automobiles, and missiles. In 1960 Getting became the first president of the Aerospace Corporation, a nonprofit organization that was created to apply modern scientific and technological advances to improving national security. Along with Bradford Parkinson and other researchers, he helped the U.S. military develop and perfect GPS.

Getting died on October 11, 2003, in Coronado, California. His many awards include the Draper Prize from the National Academy of Engineering. In 2004 he was inducted into the National Inventors Hall of Fame. Also in 2004 one of the twenty-four active GPS satellites was fitted with an engraved plate in his honor that reads, "Lighthouses in the Sky, Serving All Mankind."

around Earth. The first manmade satellite, *Sputnik*, was launched into orbit by scientists in the Soviet Union in 1957. The United States responded with its own successful launch the following year. Once these early satellites were in orbit, scientists and engineers noticed that they could track their position by listening to changes in the frequency of the radio signals they transmitted. Since the satellites' paths were known and remained constant, it soon became clear that their radio signals could be used as a navigation tool.

Two engineers at the U.S. Department of Defense, Ivan Getting (1912–2003) and Bradford Parkinson (1935–), led the effort to create a satellite-based source of continuous navigation information. The original idea was to develop a system for guiding missiles and other weapons to hit military targets. The project, called Navigation Signal Timing and Ranging (NAVSTAR), received approval in 1973. The first NAVSTAR satellite was launched into orbit in 1978, and ten more satellites were placed in orbit by 1985.

A rocket launches to take a NAVSTAR satellite into space. By 1994, 24 navigational satellites orbited Earth.

Work on the NAVSTAR system continued until the last of twenty-four navigational satellites was launched into orbit in 1994. By the time the U.S. government officially declared the system operational on April 27, 1995, it had cost more than $10 billion to develop and build. The U.S. Air Force was designated to handle ongoing management of the system. The operations and control center for the NAVSTAR program was established at Schriever Air Force Base in Colorado.

GPS Available to the Public

The air force was placed in charge of NAVSTAR because of the program's many military applications. The satellite navigation system could be used to plot targets for missile launches, coordinate troop movements, conduct surveillance operations, and much more. But it soon became apparent that satellite navigation had important nonmilitary applications as well. A commercial airline disaster helped convince President Ronald Reagan to make the NAVSTAR system available for civilian use. On September 1, 1983, a Korean Air Lines passenger jet was shot down by Soviet fighter planes after a navigational error caused it to stray into Soviet air space. All 269 people on board were killed, including a member of the U.S. Congress. President Reagan thought that satellite navigation data might have prevented the tragedy.

When the NAVSTAR system was first made available to the public in 1983, it became known by the more general term *Global Positioning System*, or GPS. Many people welcomed the opportunity to use the satellites to improve air,

GPS Declassified

In 2000 the U.S. government declassified GPS and made the most accurate navigation information available to nonmilitary users. President Bill Clinton made the following statement on May 1, 2000:

Today, I am pleased to announce that the United States will stop the intentional degradation of the Global Positioning System (GPS) signals available to the public beginning at midnight tonight. We call this degradation feature Selective Availability (SA). This will mean that civilian users of GPS will be able to pinpoint locations up to ten times more accurately than they do now. GPS is a dual-use, satellite-based system that provides accurate location and timing data to users worldwide.... It benefits users around the world in many different applications, including air, road, marine, and rail navigation, telecommunications, emergency response, oil exploration, mining, and many more. Civilian users will realize a dramatic improvement in GPS accuracy with the discontinuation of SA....This increase in accuracy will allow new GPS applications to emerge and continue to enhance the lives of people around the world.

Quoted in Federal Aviation Administration, "Navigation Services," Federal Aviation Administration, May 1, 2000, www.faa.gov/about/office_org/headquarters_offices/ato/service_units/techops/navservices/gnss/gps/policy/presidential/index.cfm.

land, and sea navigation. Countless inventors and entrepreneurs went to work to develop GPS receivers for commercial and recreational use. But some people expressed concerns about making GPS navigational data available to anyone. They worried that enemies of the United States could use the system for military purposes and thus compromise national security.

To address this concern, the U.S. Department of Defense came up with a program called Selective Availability (SA). The agency intentionally degraded the quality of the satellite signal it made available to civilian users, while it gave authorized military users access to the highest-quality signal. As a result of SA, military GPS units were accurate to between 3 feet (1m) and 50 feet (15m), while civilian GPS receivers were only accurate to within 100 feet (30m). Despite the reduced accuracy, GPS proved to be extremely popular among civilian users, and commercial applications for satellite navigation technology developed rapidly. By 2000 nonmilitary users of GPS outnumbered military users one hundred to one.

In recognition of this changing reality, President Bill Clinton announced that the U.S. military would end SA in May 2000. When the signal was no longer degraded, GPS receivers around the world were suddenly accurate to within about 10 feet (3m). "Originally developed by the Department of Defense as a military system, GPS has become a global utility," Clinton explained. "This increase in accuracy will allow new GPS applications to emerge and continue to enhance the lives of people around the world."[3]

CHAPTER 2

How the Global Positioning System Works

The Global Positioning System (GPS) consists of three main components: satellites in space, monitoring and control stations on the ground, and GPS receiver units that interpret and use the satellite signals for navigation. The satellite component of GPS involves a network or "constellation" of twenty-four satellites arranged in carefully controlled, evenly spaced orbits about 12,000 miles (19,312km) above Earth. This high orbit—about fifty times more distant than the typical orbit of the International Space Station—keeps the satellites far outside Earth's atmosphere. As a result, they circle the planet in stable, predictable arcs that follow the principles of mathematics. Their orbits are arranged so that at least four—and usually between five and eight—satellites are visible from any given spot on Earth at one time. The satellites travel at about 7,000 miles per hour (11,265kmh) and make a complete trip around Earth every twelve hours.

Each satellite is about 17 feet (5.2m) long and weighs between 2,000 and 3,000 pounds (907kg and 1,361kg). Much of its size can be attributed to the two large solar panels that extend outward from its sides and collect energy from the sun. The electrical system inside a satellite depends on solar power to operate, although it is equipped with a battery backup in case of a solar eclipse. Each satellite also has small rocket boosters that can be activated from Earth to make corrections to its orbital path, which may change slightly over time due to the gravitational pull of the moon or sun. In addition, every satellite is equipped with an antenna that allows it to receive and broadcast radio signals to Earth.

Atomic Clocks

Another important piece of equipment onboard a GPS satellite is an extremely precise timekeeping device called an atomic clock. Accurate measurements of time are essential to GPS navigation. Just as the marine chronometer revolutionized ocean exploration and the timing of radio signals made LORAN possible, the atomic clock is vital to the usefulness of GPS.

Since GPS satellites travel in predictable orbits, it is possible to know the position of each satellite at any given moment. The radio signals broadcast by the satellites travel at the speed of light, or 186,000 miles per second (299,338 kmps). By timing exactly how long it takes for a certain satellite's signal to reach a GPS receiver on Earth, it is possible to calculate the distance from that satellite to a person or object on Earth.

The atomic clocks onboard GPS satellites provide the precision timing needed to perform these calculations. Atoms are the smallest and most basic unit of all matter. An atom consists of a central nucleus that is made up of protons and neutrons and surrounded by a cloud of electrons. Every chemical element that exists on Earth has a unique atom with a

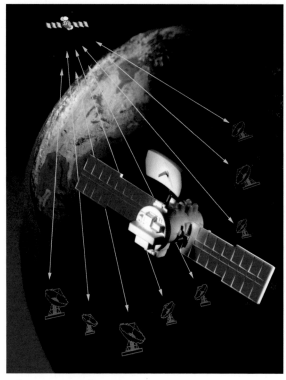

A "constellation" of 24 satellites send signals to control stations on Earth. The signals are then interpreted for navigation.

BITS & BYTES

1 second every 100,000 years

Accuracy of the atomic clocks on GPS satellites.

Atomic clocks were developed in the mid-twentieth century. They are able to tell the most precise time and enable accurate measurements.

different number of protons. The atoms of any element give off waves of electromagnetic energy in a specific frequency. A scientific process called magnetic resonance can be used to measure this frequency. Since the natural atomic frequency of different elements is known and does not change, it can be used to measure time in tiny increments.

The atomic clocks onboard GPS satellites are based on the atomic resonance frequency of the metallic element cesium. The clock itself consists of a vacuum tube or cavity containing a gas of cesium atoms, an infrared laser beam that makes the atoms move or oscillate, and a detector that measures their frequency. These clocks are among the most accurate time-keeping devices ever invented. A cesium atomic clock built by the U.S. National Institute of Standards and Technology is used to maintain the world's official, or standard, time. As of 2005, it was so accurate that it would not gain or lose a second in 60 million years.

Satellite Signals and Monitoring Stations

The exact time, as determined by a satellite's onboard atomic clock, is part of the radio signal that each GPS satellite transmits back to Earth. All twenty-four satellites in the GPS constellation broadcast a low-power (50-watt), high-frequency (1575.42 MHz) signal simultaneously. In addition to the current date and time, this signal includes codes that identify which satellite transmitted it. It also contains an up-to-date ephemeris, which is a sort of table or almanac of orbital data. The ephemeris tells the location of all the satellites at any given time.

Control stations on Earth constantly track the GPS satellites in orbit and monitor their radio signals. These monitoring stations communicate with the satellites as needed to adjust their orbits, synchronize their atomic clocks, and update navigational information. This constant attention prevents the system from gradually losing its accuracy over time.

A man and woman monitor satellites from a ground station. There are several monitoring stations around the world.

Of course, the monitoring stations are also capable of making changes that reduce the accuracy of the system. For example, the U.S. government intentionally degraded the quality of navigational information available to nonmilitary users of GPS under its Selective Availability (SA) program. In the interest of national security, ground control stations interfered with the satellite signals and introduced slight errors that varied randomly. The United States ended SA in May 2000 and made the same quality of navigational information available to both civilian and military users.

GPS monitoring stations are spaced around the world so every satellite is visible to at least one station at all times. In the United States, there are GPS monitoring stations in Washington, D.C.; Hawaii; and Colorado. Other stations are located in England, Australia, Equador, Argentina, and Bahrain. In order to monitor satellites as they pass over vast expanses of ocean, several monitoring stations are located on remote islands, such as Ascension Island in the South Atlantic Ocean, Diego Garcia in the Indian Ocean, and Kwajalein in the Pacific Ocean. The master control station, which oversees the operation of the entire Global Positioning System, is located at Schriever Air Force Base in Colorado Springs, Colorado.

Trilateration

The radio signals that are broadcast by satellites and monitored by control stations are also picked up by the antennas of electronic devices known as GPS receivers. A GPS receiver needs signals from at least four different satellites in order to determine its position. All of the satellites transmit a signal at the same time. This signal contains codes to identify which satellite it came from, ephemeris data to show the orbital location of the satellite at that moment, and the exact date and time. The GPS receiver uses the timing information to measure how long it takes the signals from different satellites to arrive. Since the signals were transmitted at the same time, the

TRILATERATION

GPS systems use trilateration to locate the exact position of a receiver. The receiver uses information encoded in the radio signal of a satellite, including the satellite's location and the time, as well as the time it took to receive the signal, to calculate the distance between the two objects. By analyzing its calculated distance from at least three separate satellites, the position of the receiver can be located. Data from four satellites can ensure added accuracy and determine altitude.

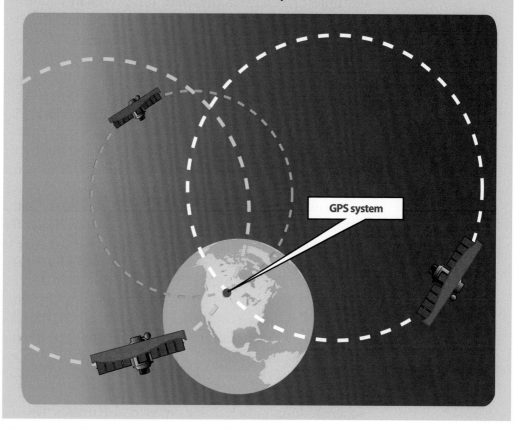

Taken from: http://www.mio.com/technology-trilateration.htm

difference in their arrival times tells how far away each satellite is from the receiver. By comparing its distance from each satellite to the known position of each satellite in orbit, a GPS receiver can calculate its own location with great accuracy.

The mathematical method that a GPS receiver uses to find its location based on its distance from satellites is called trilateration. Trilateration involves using the known locations of at least three objects to figure out the unknown location of another object. As an example, say that Joe wants to figure out where he is in the United States using trilateration. He knows that he is 780 miles (1,255km) from Dallas, Texas. With this information, Joe draws a huge circle with a diameter of 780 miles (1,255km) around Dallas on a map. Joe also knows that he is 730 miles (1,175km) from Detroit, Michigan. This information allows Joe to draw a second large circle on his map with Detroit as its center. Now Joe knows that he must be at one of the two points where the Dallas and Detroit circles overlap. Finally, Joe knows that he is 680 miles (1,094km) from Miami, Florida. This piece of information eliminates one of the two possible points on the map and tells Joe that he is in Atlanta, Georgia.

Calculating a location based on satellite signals works the same way, but in three dimensions. Instead of creating a flat circle on a map, knowing the distance from a GPS receiver to a satellite creates a large sphere. For example, say Joe now has a GPS receiver that tells him that he is 10,000 miles (16,093km) from satellite one. This information puts Joe's location somewhere on the surface of a giant sphere that extends 10,000 miles (16,093km) from satellite one. Then Joe's receiver gets a signal from satellite two, which it finds is 15,000 miles (24,140km) away from Joe's location. This information creates a second sphere around satellite two, which intersects with the first sphere to form a circle. If Joe's receiver determines that satellite three is 20,000 miles (32,187km) away, this additional information creates a third sphere that intersects with the others in just two points. One of these points will be in space, so Joe can eliminate that result and pinpoint his location on Earth. A GPS receiver can thus calculate its position in latitude and longitude using data from three satellites, but a fourth is needed to determine its elevation.

GPS Receivers

In order to perform the complicated mathematical calculations required for trilateration, GPS receivers are fairly sophisticated electronic devices. Although there are many different kinds of GPS receivers, they all work in basically the same way. They all have antennas to receive radio signals from GPS satellites and screens to display information. They also have microprocessors, which are like tiny computers, to interpret the information contained in those signals and use it to calculate a position.

When a GPS receiver is turned on, it immediately begins scanning for satellite signals. Its antenna recognizes the digital pattern transmitted by GPS satellites and locks onto the signals of at least four satellites. Part of the signal broadcast by the satellites is the exact date and time—accurate to

Inside a GPS Receiver

A GPS receiver is a complicated electronic device that contains many parts. One important part is an antenna for receiving radio signals from GPS satellites. The antenna must be able to pick up the frequencies used to transmit GPS data, and it also must be able to compensate for interference from the user and from the unit's own internal electronic parts. A GPS receiver also contains a radio frequency integrated circuit to amplify and decode the various parts of the satellite signal, including satellite identification codes, time and date information, and ephemeris data. A GPS receiver also contains a quartz clock that is continually reset to match the precise time kept by the atomic clocks onboard the GPS satellites. In addition, a GPS receiver contains a microprocessor that inputs the time and position information from different satellites and performs the necessary calculations to figure out its exact location in latitude and longitude. Finally, a GPS receiver has electronic memory to hold map application software and a display screen to interface with the user.

A GPS receiver gets radio signals from GPS satellites and displays the information on its screen.

the nanosecond—as determined by the satellites' onboard atomic clocks. The GPS receiver uses this information to synchronize its own internal clock with the ones on the satellites. Since an atomic clock costs between fifty thousand dollars and one hundred thousand dollars, it would be far too expensive to put one in every handheld GPS receiver. Instead, the receivers use ordinary quartz clocks and constantly reset them to match the time transmitted by the satellites. As a result, GPS receivers are nearly as accurate as atomic clocks, and any two receivers in the world will have the same time to within milliseconds.

Another valuable part of the satellite signal is the ephemeris data that show the position of every satellite in the constellation at that moment. A GPS receiver stores an almanac in its memory that lists the orbital position of all the satellites. Like the time and date, this information is constantly updated from the satellite signals. Whenever the monitoring stations adjust the orbit of a satellite, the changes are immediately transmitted to all GPS receivers as part of the satellites' signals.

If a GPS receiver knows the exact time and the position of at least four satellites, it can calculate its own position. First, the receiver measures the delay between the time each satellite broadcasts its signal and the time it receives that signal. This tiny amount of time is how long it took the signal to travel to the receiver's location on Earth. Next, the GPS receiver multiplies the signal's travel time by the speed of light, which gives it the distance to each satellite. Finally, using trilateration to compare its distance from several satellites, the receiver determines its location.

Maps and Routing

Providing information about a user's current position is an important function of a GPS receiver. That information becomes even more useful, however, when it is incorporated into mapping software applications to show geographical features of the surrounding area. This allows users to view their current position in relation to streets, businesses,

A GPS receiver in a car shows directions for the driver to follow.

Becoming a Surveyor or Cartographer

Job Description: Surveyors and cartographers are responsible for measuring and mapping land areas, defining legal boundaries, and analyzing geographic data. Surveyors often use GPS receivers to provide reference points for precise measurements. Cartographers often use satellite data when collecting, analyzing, and displaying location information on maps.

Education: A bachelor's degree in cartography, geography, surveying, engineering, or computer science is strongly preferred.

Qualifications: Most states require surveyors and cartographers to be licensed through the National Council of Examiners for Engineering and Surveying. Earning a license requires passing written examinations and working under the supervision of an experienced surveyor for four years. Both jobs require good spatial awareness, knowledge of geography and mathematics, and computer skills.

Salary: $51,000 to $53,000 per year

natural features, and other landmarks. Most GPS receivers have internal memory that allows them to store a variety of digital maps. Others come with plug-in cartridges that hold large amounts of map data. Many GPS receivers can also connect to the Internet, either through a computer or via a wireless connection, to gain access to additional maps and information online.

By combining location data from satellites with geographic features from maps, GPS receivers gain the ability to perform several important functions. For instance, most GPS receivers can track real-time changes in a user's position. They maintain continuous communication with the satellites, update their location data regularly, and display the changes on a map. As users move, the receivers trace their route and provide information about the direction of travel, speed, distance, and elapsed time of the trip. Many GPS units allow users to enter the map coordinates for a specific location—known as a waypoint—and plot a route to get there from their current location. Most receivers also have the capacity to store the coordinates for a waypoint in their memory to enable users to return to it later.

IMPROVING ACCURACY WITH DIFFERENTIAL GPS

The Differential GPS system is made up of stationary (unmoving) reference stations where GPS receivers collect data from NAVSTAR satellites. Because the orbits of the satellites are known, and the locations of the reference stations are constant, the reference receivers can detect delays. The reference stations send corrections to all surrounding GPS receivers, so that they can auto-correct the information from delayed satellite signals.

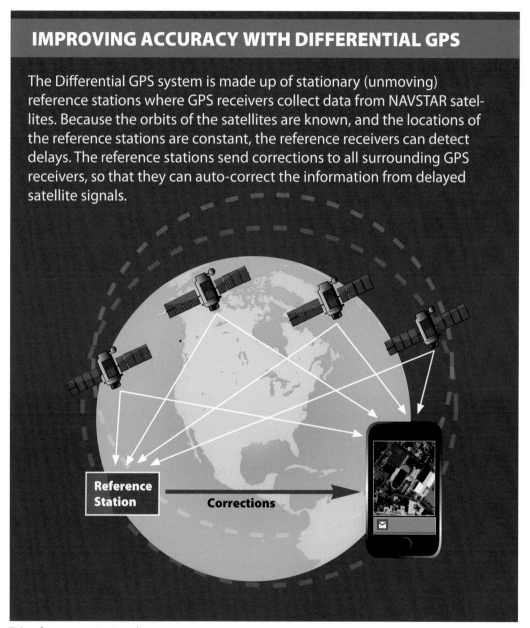

Reference Station

Corrections

Taken from www.circuitstoday.com

GPS receivers vary greatly in the maps and coordinate grids they support, their capacity for storing waypoints and plotting routes, and their ability to provide navigational statistics like direction, speed, and distance traveled. There is also a wide variation among units in terms of size, weight, battery life, display screen, data entry keys, and voice navigation capability. In addition, different models of GPS receivers are built for specific applications or activities. Sturdy, lightweight, handheld units are marketed to outdoors enthusiasts, for example, while units with large display screens and voice navigation capability are designed for use in cars.

Differential GPS

Besides offering different features, GPS receivers also vary in their accuracy. After the U.S. government stopped degrading the quality of the satellite signal available to civilian users in 2000, most GPS units on the market were accurate to within 50 feet (15m). This level of accuracy is acceptable for most recreational uses of the technology. But applications such as weapons targeting, surveying, marine navigation, and air traffic control require more precise positional data.

In addition to variations among systems, a number of factors can interfere with satellite signals and reduce the accuracy of typical GPS receivers. When satellite signals pass through the atmospheric layer known as the ionosphere, for instance, they may travel slower than the speed of light. If the signal is delayed in reaching Earth, then it introduces errors into the time and distance calculations made by GPS receivers. Since the amount of the delay varies depending on where the receiver is located on Earth, it is difficult to correct for it. In addition, radio signals from satellites tend to bounce off of tall objects on Earth, such as skyscrapers or canyon walls. Any reflection of the signal also introduces delays that can cause navigational errors. Finally, satellites occasionally transmit inaccurate information about their orbital position.

To correct for such errors and make GPS receivers more accurate, U.S. government scientists and engineers came up with a supplementary, or additional, navigational system called Differential GPS (DGPS). It consists of a network of land-based radio antennas that receive signals from GPS satellites. Since these receiving stations are stationary and know their own locations, they are able to calculate the exact degree of inaccuracy—or differential—in the satellite signals. The antennas then broadcast radio signals of their own

Skyscrapers can interfere with radio signals from satellites. This can create navigational errors in GPS receivers.

that provide correction information to DGPS receivers in the local area. This information makes GPS receivers that are equipped with a differential beacon antenna much more accurate than ordinary GPS receivers. In fact, most DGPS receivers are accurate to within 10 to 15 feet (3m to 4.5m).

The main DGPS correction service is operated by the U.S. Coast Guard. It consists of a network of more than sixty differential beacon transmitters along the coasts of the U.S.

mainland, the coasts of Alaska and Hawaii, on the shores of the Great Lakes, and along the Mississippi River. Each beacon transmits correction information to DGPS receivers within about 200 miles (322km) of its location. Although the Coast Guard's Differential GPS was originally intended to provide more accurate navigational information for ships, it has proven valuable to land-based GPS users as well.

Wide Area Augmentation System

The usefulness of Differential GPS in marine and land navigation helped convince the Federal Aviation Administration (FAA) and the Department of Transportation (DOT) to develop a similar program to increase the accuracy of GPS for air navigation. This program, known as the Wide Area Augmentation System (WAAS), consists of about twenty-five ground-monitoring stations spread across the United States. These stations listen to GPS satellite signals and compute the degree of inaccuracy at their locations. Two master stations, located on the Atlantic and Pacific coasts, use data collected from the monitoring stations to create a correction message. This message is relayed to two geostationary satellites, which have a fixed orbital position above the equator. These satellites broadcast the correction message to all WAAS-enabled GPS receivers. Using WAAS can increase the accuracy of GPS navigational data to within less than 10 feet (3m).

In addition to increased accuracy, WAAS offers several advantages over Differential GPS. By using satellites to transmit signals, it provides correction information to GPS users farther inland and farther offshore than DGPS. It also transmits that information in a format that can be understood by regular GPS receivers, so using it does not require special equipment. On the other hand, WAAS does have a few disadvantages. The system was developed primarily for air navigation in order to make GPS meet the FAA's stringent requirements for positional accuracy. As a result, land-based users in North America sometimes have trouble receiving signals from the geostationary WAAS satellites when tall buildings or mountain ranges obstruct their view of the southern horizon.

Although WAAS was still in its final stages of development and testing as of 2010, it held a great deal of promise for increasing the precision of GPS technology. In recognition of this fact, several other governments launched programs to develop their own GPS correction systems. Japan introduced the Multi-Functional Satellite Augmentation System (MSAS), for example, and the European Union established the Euro Geostationary Navigation Overlay Service (EGNOS). Over time, such programs are expected to make the most accurate position data available to GPS users around the world.

CHAPTER 3

Uses of Global Positioning System Technology

Hundreds of different applications exist for the Global Positioning System (GPS), with more appearing every day. "Along with the Internet, GPS is one of the great enabling technologies of our globalized age, and we have only begun to mine its seemingly limitless applications,"[4] writes Andrew Marshall in *Time International*. The most popular uses of GPS technology include location assistance (determining one's own position), navigation (plotting a route to a desired location), tracking (monitoring the location of a GPS-equipped person, animal, or object), mapping (compiling geographic data and route information), and keeping time (using satellite signals for precise timekeeping). The most commonly used application of GPS technology is navigation on land, in the air, and in the water.

With these basic functions, GPS has proven useful in a wide variety of settings. The U.S. military, for instance, uses the technology for surveillance and weapons targeting. Among the many commercial applications of GPS, construction crews use it to survey building sites, while delivery services use it to plan efficient routes. Scientists use it in global climate change research, ecosystem mapping, and natural resource management. GPS technology has also found a range of applications in outdoor recreation, from hiking, biking, fishing, and boating to the popular treasure-hunt game known as geocaching. As the usefulness of these specialized systems became clear, GPS receivers made their way into cars and mobile phones as well.

Military Uses

GPS technology was originally developed with potential military uses in mind. The first major test of the system in a combat situation occurred during the 1991 Persian Gulf War. During this conflict, a U.S.-led coalition of multinational troops forced the country of Iraq to end its occupation of neighboring Kuwait. This effort was greatly aided by the U.S. military's decision to equip its land vehicles and ground forces with GPS receivers. GPS enabled them to navigate with confidence, even when it was dark outside or visibility was

A man attaches a smart weapon to a jet fighter. GPS technology first used during the 1991 Persian Gulf War allowed for more precise targeting.

limited. In fact, the new technology proved so valuable to U.S. forces fighting in the deserts of Iraq and Kuwait that it revolutionized military operations from that time forward. "GPS satellites enabled coalition forces to navigate, maneuver, and fire with unprecedented accuracy in the vast desert terrain almost 24 hours per day despite difficult conditions—frequent sandstorms, few paved roads, no vegetative cover, and few natural landmarks,"[5] explain the authors of *The Global Positioning System: Assessing National Policies.*

Thanks to the emergence of GPS technology, the American troops always knew their exact positions, and U.S. military leaders could track the location of fighting units and plan the routes of supply convoys. GPS capability proved so popular among coalition troops that the number of handheld receivers issued to American soldiers grew from one thousand at the beginning of the war to nearly nine thousand by the end of the war.

One of the most remarkable images to emerge from the Gulf War was that of U.S. military aircraft hitting impossibly small targets—such as a pipe on the roof of an Iraqi factory—with precision-guided missiles. Viewers of war footage aired on television news programs learned that GPS technology was partly responsible for this feat. Military leaders used satellite images to locate, identify, and track hostile targets and then programmed the coordinates into weapon-guidance systems. Cruise missiles, artillery shells, and bombs were equipped with multichannel GPS receivers that constantly calculated their positions while in flight, thus allowing them to hit targets with great accuracy from long distances.

The military applications of GPS technology continued to expand following the Gulf War. The systems have proven useful to U.S. Navy vessels in organizing rendezvous at sea as well as in minesweeping operations. GPS data is also vital to military search and rescue and emergency response teams. Airplanes, ships, vehicles, and combat troops are routinely equipped with radios that feature integrated GPS locator beacons. When activated in an emergency, these beacons provide rescue teams with precise location coordinates for downed pilots or combat casualties, allowing them to respond quickly and save lives. Finally, GPS data is invaluable to military planners in creating up-to-date maps to determine the location of targets, the placement of weapons and personnel, the most efficient supply routes, and the most effective defense strategies. In the future, the military applications of GPS may evolve to include guidance and tracking devices small enough to fit into a boot or a bullet. "In a progression from hitting a specific building to hitting a specific room, the next generation will, among other things, turn the foot soldier into a precision strike weapon, able to… fire guided bullets at targets like would-be snipers before they have a chance to fire at him,"[6] explains J.R. Wilson in *Military & Aerospace Electronics* magazine.

Commercial and Municipal Uses

The military applications of GPS generated a great deal of media coverage during the Persian Gulf War and afterward. This attention led to a significant increase in civilian interest in and uses for the exciting new technology. Surveyors and mapmakers were among the earliest enterprises to adopt GPS for commercial use. They use satellite positioning data to confirm their manual measurements and enhance digital maps. GPS reduces the setup time needed for surveys, and

A man works in the Chunnel, the underground tunnel connecting England and France. GPS technology was used in constructing the Chunnel.

Civilian GPS and U.S. Policy

As people around the world grow ever more dependent upon GPS technology to conduct their daily activities, some critics have expressed concern about what would happen if the U.S. government someday decided to block civilian access to satellite navigation. After all, the United States has independent authority and control over the most prevalent and accurate system in the world. But most government agencies are very reassuring about the continued availability of the technology.

The official U.S. policy on space-based positioning, navigation, and timing services was established in 2004. It encourages the worldwide use of GPS and the innovative development of new civilian applications for GPS technology. Although the U.S. Department of Defense has the authority to maintain and operate GPS for both military and civilian use, it is required by law to provide civil GPS service "on a continuous, worldwide basis, free of direct user fees." The secretary of defense is also required to develop ways to prevent the hostile use of GPS "without unduly disrupting or degrading civilian uses."

National Executive Committee for Space-Based Positioning, Navigation, and Timing, "U.S. Space-Based PNT Policy," National Executive Committee for Space-Based Positioning, Navigation, and Timing, http://pnt .gov/policy.

high-quality professional systems can achieve accuracy to within centimeters.

Construction companies also embraced GPS technology in planning, measuring, and mapping out building sites. It is also helpful in marine surveying, dredging and waterway maintenance work, and laying of underwater cable and pipelines. One of the most famous examples of the use of GPS in a construction project is from the building of a tunnel under the English Channel linking Dover, England, to Calais, France. To build the "Chunnel," as it became known, construction crews began digging from opposite sides of the waterway. They used GPS receivers to confirm their relative positions and ensure that the two excavation sites would meet in the middle.

GPS navigation has also proven valuable to businesses and city governments that operate fleets of vehicles, such as package delivery and courier services, taxi services, garbage

GPS and National Security

The usefulness of GPS technology in weapons guidance led the U.S. government to limit the export of certain GPS receivers in the interest of national security in 2006. The limits apply to receivers that are capable of functioning above 60,000 feet (18,288m) of altitude and at 1,151 miles per hour (1,852kmp) and are intended to prevent their use in ballistic missiles. All civilian GPS receivers that exceed these parameters are classified as munitions and require a special export license from the U.S. Department of State.

collection enterprises, road maintenance crews, and appliance repair services. The technology enables these businesses to save time and money by planning optimal travel routes, tracking mileage and fuel economy, and providing drivers with street-by-street directions to destinations. Large companies like Federal Express and Sears have equipped their huge fleets with GPS technologies that enable a central office to track the vehicles on delivery routes and repair calls. The central office determines the safest and fastest route to a destination, assigns the nearest driver to a call, and schedules vehicle maintenance as needed.

GPS technology has also proven useful in such industries as agriculture and natural resource development and extraction. In forestry, for instance, GPS is used to pinpoint the location of stands of timber for cutting and to mark the boundaries of areas for planting. The technology is also used in the mining and oil and gas industries to create maps of sample sites, wells, and promising areas for exploration. In addition, the use of GPS in large farming operations has led to increases in agricultural efficiency and productivity. Farmers use GPS to map field boundaries, organize soil sampling, design irrigation systems, create crop plans, and guide tractors during low visibility conditions. They also use GPS to note the precise location of insect and weed infestations in order to limit the application of fertilizer and pesticides to problem areas. The information provided by GPS technology has led to higher crop yields and more environmentally responsible agricultural practices.

A number of other types of businesses have found innovative uses for GPS technology as well. For example, auto insurance and rental car companies equip vehicles with GPS in order to record mileage, speed, and routes traveled. This information enables the companies to customize the rates they charge based on actual use of the vehicles. Port authorities in some cities put GPS tracking devices on shipping containers in order to control the transportation of hazardous materials and prevent them from being taken on unapproved routes. Finally, some tourist attractions like parks, zoos, and historic sites use GPS technology to track visitors and record information about their routes and activities. Park managers can use this information in planning the expansion of popular exhibits or the addition of new signs or pathways to improve traffic patterns.

Scientific Uses

In addition to the many military and commercial uses of GPS, there are also valuable scientific applications for the technology. Oceanographers, for instance, use GPS when surveying underwater terrain and creating maps of features on the ocean floor. They also use the technology to record the precise location of underwater points of interest so they can return there later for further study. GPS-equipped buoys (anchored floats) provide data to help scientists track fluctuating sea levels, shifting currents, and changing tides. They can also relay information about environmental hazards, such as a spreading oil spill, to assist in cleanup operations.

GPS tracking systems are also used by scientists who study the earth's climate and weather. They often place GPS devices in high-altitude weather balloons that are used to monitor atmospheric conditions, such as the holes in the ozone layer above the North and South Poles. Satellite positioning data also helps scientists forecast

A high-altitude balloon is inflated prior to its flight. High-altitude balloons may carry GPS receivers to monitor atmospheric conditions.

and track hurricanes, typhoons, and other storms. On the ground, geologists use GPS technology to create detailed maps of the earth's crust that include the precise locations of fault lines (cracks in the earth's crust). By measuring slight movements along fault lines, they can study the buildup of pressure that leads to earthquakes. GPS satellites are also used to collect data on the electromagnetic radiation reflected from the earth's surface. By analyzing these reflected signals, scientists can gain valuable insights into changing environmental conditions, such as the amount of sea ice in the Arctic or the density of rain forest cover in Brazil.

GPS technology is also used in biology and medicine. Biologists make extensive use of GPS receivers in field studies to record the exact locations of air, soil, and water samples. They also place GPS collars on wildlife in order to track migration routes and habitat range. Similar devices are used by medical professionals to keep tabs on the location of patients suffering from dementia (disorders involving

Becoming a Geographic Information Systems Analyst or Technician

Job Description: Geographic information systems analysts and technicians are experts in the use of computer systems that collect, manipulate, analyze, and display spatial information and use it to create specialized maps.

Education: A bachelor's degree in geography or computer programming is required.

Qualifications: Knowledge of geography and cartography; an understanding of math and statistical analysis; strong computer programming skills with knowledge of two or more GIS packages as well as Macro/C/C++/Visual Basic; and experience with Oracle or other relational database management systems.

Salary: $57,900 to $66,800 per year

mental functioning). GPS tracking devices can be placed unobtrusively in a patient's shoes or clothing or be worn as a belt or bracelet. These devices give the patients more freedom to live on their own or move around outdoors because they can be found quickly if they become disoriented or lost. GPS technology has also proven useful to people with visual impairments. Using detailed maps of their neighborhood or even unfamiliar surroundings, they can program a GPS receiver to provide spoken step-by-step directions to a desired location.

Scientists and engineers also take advantage of the precise timing capability of the atomic clocks onboard GPS satellites. Since the satellites broadcast the exact time continuously—and their signals can reach even the remotest locations anywhere in the world—the atomic clocks can be used as a reference to synchronize the timing of computer networks, telecommunication services, and power-distribution facilities that are spread out over large geographic areas. Precise timing of signals through these networks helps engineers locate problem areas and fix them quickly. It also plays an important role in a variety of time-sensitive applications, such as global financial markets that open and close for trading at a specific time of day.

Using GPS for Emergencies

GPS technology also has a wide range of applications in the areas of personal safety, emergency response, search and rescue, and disaster relief. GPS receivers in cellular phones or backpacks, for instance, enable parents to know the location of their children at all times and find them if they go missing. Some parents use the technology to provide real-time information on the whereabouts of a teenage driver and alert them if their vehicle exceeds a certain speed or ventures outside of a programmable boundary. Similar equipment can be placed in pet collars to allow pet owners to track their animals and find them if they become lost. Some of the first people to take advantage of this GPS capability were hunters, who used it to follow their hunting dogs.

GPS positioning data has also proven valuable to emergency personnel like police, firefighters, and paramedics. Automated vehicle tracking systems, such as General Motors' OnStar, are able to sense when a vehicle is involved in an accident and report the location to emergency services. In addition, U.S. law requires cellular phones to be

OnStar workers monitor radio signals from satellites to help customers in an emergency.

Enhanced 911 Program

Emergency response is an important use of GPS technology. If someone gets lost, has an accident, or is the victim of a crime, a GPS-enabled communication device can give responders information about the person's location. The Federal Communications Commission (FCC) recognized this potential benefit of GPS capability when it launched the Enhanced 911 program for cellular phones in 1999. This program required every wireless phone to automatically transmit its phone number and location to a public safety answering point when the user dials 911. In order to comply with the FCC ruling, all cell phones sold in the United States have to have some GPS receiving capability built into the phone.

When someone dials 911 from a landline, the 911 operator immediately knows the address of the caller. But cell phones do not provide an address or other fixed location. Before the Enhanced 911 program took effect, a 911 operator who received a call from a cell phone only knew the location of the cell tower nearest to the caller. The Enhanced 911 program ensures that the exact coordinates of the caller's position are available to emergency responders. Although some critics worried that building GPS receivers into cell phones would create privacy issues, most users did not share these concerns. In fact, GPS navigation capability became a popular component of smartphones.

equipped with a GPS receiver that is capable of automatically relaying its position to 911 emergency operators. Once the location of an emergency has been reported, emergency personnel use GPS data to map the location, choose the fastest route given road construction and traffic conditions, and identify the closest medical facility. Meanwhile, hospital personnel can monitor ambulances, estimate their time of arrival, and prepare the equipment needed to care for the victims.

GPS technology can also help save lives during search and rescue and disaster relief operations. During natural disasters like the Indian Ocean tsunami in 2004 and Hurricane Katrina in 2005, for example, search and rescue teams used GPS maps to navigate through flooded streets and buildings because the usual landmarks had been destroyed. They also used GPS receivers to pinpoint the location of survivors and transport them to the nearest medical care. Finally, GPS technology enables aircraft to plot the boundaries of forest fires and guide firefighters to key spots in a safe and timely manner.

Land, Air, and Water Navigation

Probably the best-known application of GPS technology is land navigation. Many automobile manufacturers offer built-in satellite navigations systems as optional equipment in their new vehicles. There are also a wide variety of portable, stand-alone GPS receivers that are specifically designed for use in automobiles. All of these devices use GPS satellite signals to determine a car's position on the road. Most units are loaded with an extensive database of road maps and a searchable directory of gas stations, hotels, restaurants, and attractions that users can consult. They allow travelers to enter the street address of a home or business and obtain turn-by-turn directions to the desired location. Most built-in or in-dash navigation systems also provide real-time traffic and road construction information to drivers. Some systems even provide emergency roadside assistance services.

GPS technology is steadily increasing its role in air navigation, as well. After Selective Availability was turned off in 2000 and civilian GPS receivers became more accurate, the Federal Aviation Administration (FAA) revised its rules to allow GPS to serve as the primary means of navigation for some flights. The technology proved especially valuable in areas where ground-based air-traffic control and navigation signals could not reach, such as mid-ocean air space and other remote areas of the world. In other areas, the FAA certified GPS for use during flights guided by instrument flight rules (regulations for flying aircraft by referring only to the instrument panel for navigation) and during nonprecision approaches (which utilize fewer navigational aids than precision approaches). The agency also approved the use of certain GPS units—including those that achieved a higher degree of accuracy

BITS & BYTES

400 feet

Accuracy of the original GPS navigation information under Selective Availability.

and reliability by linking to the ground-based Wide Area Augmentation System (WAAS)—for all flights.

Reliability was the FAA's main concern about GPS navigation in the air. Agency officials worried that an error in a satellite signal, or a loss of signal, might cause GPS-dependent planes to veer off course or crash. To protect against in-flight GPS errors, they instituted a mandatory program called Receiver Autonomous Integrity Monitoring (RAIM). RAIM ensures that aircraft GPS receivers maintain contact with at least five satellites and sound an alarm if it detects one or more satellites transmitting questionable data. Most light aircraft are equipped with GPS units that show the plane's position and altitude on a map during flight. Pilots can also program the device to display a flight plan and show the plane's deviation from the selected route.

With the protection offered by RAIM and the ever-increasing accuracy of GPS technology, the FAA eventually determined that GPS could serve as the primary means of navigation for all aircraft. The agency planned to phase out ground-based systems beginning in 2011, when the U.S. government began replacing older satellites with updated GPS III models. The GPS III satellites will feature five hundred times greater signal power than earlier models and will be fully compatible with global navigation systems under development in Europe, Russia, and elsewhere. Many observers predict that moving to GPS navigation will lead to more efficient use of air space, fewer flight delays, increased flight safety, and savings in fuel consumption.

GPS navigation offers many of the same benefits when it is used on water. The technology enables marine mapmakers to note the precise location of shallow areas and underwater obstacles. Boaters equipped with GPS receivers can determine the position of their vessels on these maps, as well as their speed and heading. GPS thus makes it possible for boaters to maneuver safely in narrow channels and busy harbors. They can also navigate more easily in open waters during periods of low visibility from darkness, fog, bad weather, or rough seas. GPS navigation systems eliminate many of the hazards that once faced ships at sea. "Unlike the danger and uncertainty faced by many seamen in past centuries, navigating the world's waters today is a lot like playing a video game on a computer screen," writes Linda Williams in her book *Great Inventions: Navigational Aids.* "Gone are the days of leaving family and friends to explore uncharted waters with a good chance of never returning. With satellite navigation and positioning networks, knowledgeable navigators have little reason to become lost."[7]

Outdoor Recreation

Millions of people around the world use GPS navigation technology to enhance their recreational activities and ensure that they always find their way home again. There are portable, handheld GPS receivers available on the market that are geared toward specific activities, such as hiking, biking, hunting, fishing, boating, and golfing. There are also a wide variety of general-purpose GPS-enabled devices, such as cellular phones, that can be used for outdoor navigation. The most useful units have the ability to record the path a user follows to reach a remote location. The user can refer to this route information—known as a track log or breadcrumb trail—to retrace their steps back to their starting point. This feature enables users to navigate through dense forests, featureless deserts, twisting canyons, and other potentially confusing terrain without becoming lost.

The best GPS receivers for land-based outdoor recreation also come equipped with detailed topographical maps that include trail information. These maps provide hikers, mountain bikers, snowmobilers, and other outdoor enthusiasts with access to areas that are not accessible by road. Nautical maps are useful for canoeists and kayakers who need to navigate confusing waterways or networks of islands. GPS navigation also helps boaters travel safely in coastal areas during periods of bad weather or poor visibility. Hunters and fishermen make use of the technology to mark the location of blinds or favorite fishing holes so they can return to them later.

GPS has even gained popularity among avid golfers. Portable GPS units can be carried in golf bags or mounted in golf carts. These units are loaded with maps of favorite golf courses. Golfers who utilize GPS technology can see

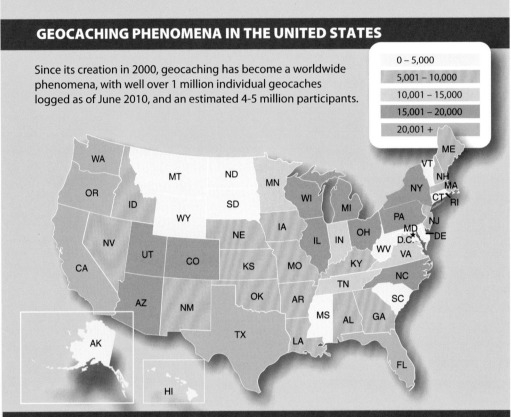

GEOCACHING PHENOMENA IN THE UNITED STATES

Since its creation in 2000, geocaching has become a worldwide phenomena, with well over 1 million individual geocaches logged as of June 2010, and an estimated 4-5 million participants.

0 – 5,000	
5,001 – 10,000	
10,001 – 15,000	
15,001 – 20,000	
20,001 +	

GEOCACHING AROUND THE WORLD

Country	# of Geocaches	Country	# of Geocaches
Antarctica	34	Iran	17
Australia	23,930	Japan	4,948
Brazil	512	Kenya	39
Canada	89,439	Russia	109
China	292	Sweden	27,221
Egypt	127	United Kingdom	63,239
Germany	141,324	United States	573,638
India	94		

Taken from: Data found at www.geocaching.com

their exact location on the course, measure the precise distance from their ball to the hole, and use this information to choose clubs and plan shots. Many golf enthusiasts have found that GPS improves both their play and their enjoyment of the game.

As the use of GPS receivers in the outdoors gained popularity, some users came up with new activities to take advantage of the technology. One of the first GPS-specific activities to appear was geocaching. "Geo" stands for geographical coordinates, or latitude and longitude, and a cache is a hidden storage location. Geocaching is like a high-tech scavenger hunt in which participants use GPS receivers to find hidden treasures. The game originated in May 2000 with Dave Ulmer, a GPS enthusiast. He hid a container full of trinkets in the woods outside of Portland, Oregon, posted the coordinates on the Internet, and invited others to find it. Geocaching caught on quickly and became popular all over the world.

Ten years later there were hundreds of Internet sites dedicated to geocaching. Anyone with a GPS receiver could log into a site like Geocaching.com, select a cache from a list, enter the coordinates into their GPS unit, and follow the route to find the treasure. The rules in geocaching require participants to bring a trinket of their own to exchange for an item in a cache, so that there will always be something for later arrivals to find. There is also a variation of the game called geodashing, which is a sort of outdoor adventure race in which participants use GPS coordinates to locate a series of checkpoints as quickly as possible.

Another popular outdoor activity that grew out of GPS technology involves visiting places that have interesting geographical coordinates, like the line at 45 degrees north latitude that is exactly halfway between the equator and the North Pole. Many people enjoy exploring some of the fourteen thousand spots on Earth where the degrees of latitude and longitude intersect. These locations, known as degrees of confluence, exist at coordinates that are round numbers with no decimal places. The Web site Confluence.org is dedicated to degrees of confluence, and visitors to the site can record

Two players talk during a high-tech scavenger hunt called geocaching, which uses GPS receivers to guide players to hidden treasure.

information about their visits to various locations and post photographs.

GPS units have also emerged as a valuable resource in tourism. In addition to finding routes to hotels, restaurants, or attractions in unfamiliar cities, some users download special maps and information known as geotours. These lists of coordinates for interesting sites and routes from one site to the next turn GPS receivers into virtual guidebooks that help travelers explore new places. In addition, some people use their GPS units on their way to vacation destinations to see what interesting features they might be flying over. There are a number of Web sites that provide the coordinates for points of interest that can be seen from the air, such as Niagara Falls in New York or Meteor Crater in Arizona. The rules for GPS use by passengers on commercial flights vary, however, so users should always consult the airline first.

Finally, some people use GPS technology closer to home to create their own digital maps of local cities, neighborhoods, parks, or the countryside. They simply bring along a GPS receiver whenever they take a walk, drive, ride a bike, get on a boat, or go on any other excursion, and record data about their chosen routes and any interesting features they encounter along the way. By combining information about various journeys, they can build personalized maps that include far more detail than would be available on commercial maps. Some GPS enthusiasts share their original maps with other users online.

CHAPTER 4

Impact of Global Positioning System Technology

The many applications of the Global Positioning System (GPS) have made the technology an indispensable part of modern life. During the relatively short time since the full constellation of GPS satellites became operational in 1995, GPS has revolutionized navigation and fundamentally transformed the way individuals and businesses perform many basic functions. In 2009 a panel of experts from the British Science Association ranked GPS at the top of its list of ten inventions that have most changed the world throughout history. "Twenty years ago, GPS was just a promise," writes Jules McNeff in a 2010 article for *GPS World* magazine. "It had not contributed to victory on the battlefield; it had not revolutionized earth science nor changed the way businesses and people conduct their daily activities. Now it has done all of that. It has awakened a global awareness of precise and ubiquitous position and time and of their value as essential elements of every human endeavor."[8]

While GPS technology has made a tremendous impact on various aspects of life, its rapidly expanding use has also exposed certain problems and limitations. Satellite signals are subject to interference from atmospheric conditions,

GPS technology has had many effects, from directing tourists to popular sites to helping farmers map fields.

physical obstacles, or competing radio signals, for example, and GPS receivers occasionally fail. Scientists and engineers are working to overcome such problems and modernize the system in order to reduce the potential for serious disruptions to GPS service in the future.

Revolutionizing Transportation

The impact of GPS technology has been so widespread and varied that it can be difficult to remember what life was like without it. Before GPS navigation systems became standard equipment in millions of automobiles, for instance, travelers routinely visited travel agents, collected paper maps, and consulted guidebooks before heading off on a long car trip. If they became lost in an unfamiliar city, they had to stop to ask for directions. If their planned route was blocked by an accident or road construction, they had to guess at the best way to navigate around the problem. If they wanted to grab a bite to eat or fill up the gas tank, they had to get off the highway at the nearest exit and hope to find a restaurant or gas station. The invention of portable GPS units for automobiles solved all of these problems. Travelers gained access to location and route information, maps of local roads and businesses, and street-by-street directions in their vehicles whenever they needed it. GPS navigation thus revolutionized car trips by saving time, eliminating the need for intensive planning, and reducing reliance on others for direction.

Automobile travel is just one of the many facets of transportation that has been transformed by GPS technology. In addition to providing drivers with navigation data, GPS has also made it possible to route commercial vehicles—such as delivery trucks and road maintenance crews—more efficiently from a central location. Municipal governments and businesses alike have taken advantage of this capability of GPS technology to increase employees' productivity and reduce fuel consumption. A 2008 study commissioned by the communications company Motorola found that businesses achieved significant time and cost savings when they used GPS technologies in their vehicle fleets. On average, companies reduced the distance their vehicles traveled by 231 miles (372km) per week, which translated into an annual fuel savings of $51,500 per year. Employees also saved an average of fifty-four minutes per day in travel time. The associated increase in productivity translated to an average reduction in labor costs of $5.4 million per year. In addition, the companies surveyed reported that route efficiencies led to improvements in their on-time performance and customer service.

Public transportation authorities also use GPS to track the location of trains, buses, subway trains, and other mass-transit vehicles. The technology has contributed to improvements in route planning and on-time performance. In the case of railroads, for example, GPS provides centralized command-and-control centers with precise location, speed, and direction information for every train. This information helps railroad managers maintain smooth traffic flow, prevent collisions, minimize delays, and arrange track maintenance. It also aids passengers by increasing the reliability of schedules, which makes it easier to make connections with other modes of transportation. Most rail lines use Differential GPS (DGPS), which augments satellite signals with radio signals from ground stations in order to provide greater accuracy. If two trains are running on parallel tracks, DGPS enables dispatchers to determine which track is occupied by which train. It also helps dispatchers track trains when they pass through tunnels or behind mountains or buildings.

GPS technology has had a similar impact on the safety and efficiency of marine transportation. The International Maritime Organization has implemented a GPS-based method of controlling boat traffic called the Automatic Identification System (AIS). AIS transponders (transmitter-receivers that, when they receive certain signals, automatically send out signals of their own) send out radio signals that identify all the ships in a certain area, give their exact geographic locations, and provide information about their cargo. This automated service helps commercial ships navigate safely in busy waterways and enables a greater number of ships to operate within a given area. It also increases the security of ports by providing port authorities with real-time information about commercial vessels and their contents.

Bolstering the Global Economy

A less-obvious area in which GPS technology has made a tremendous impact is the global economy. The precision timing capability of GPS plays an important role in many economic activities. The atomic clocks onboard GPS satellites keep time that is accurate to within billionths of a second. The exact time is part of the radio signals that the satellites broadcast continuously to receivers all over the world. Governments and businesses use these precise time signals to synchronize all sorts of information exchanges that occur on a global basis.

GPS time synchronization is vital to the operation of electrical power grids, communication systems, computer networks, and financial transactions that extend over large geographical areas. By synchronizing the time at widely dispersed base stations, for instance, cellular telephone and data networks enable more mobile devices to share limited frequencies. Radio services that broadcast digital signals from different stations also use GPS timing to synchronize their transmissions. This ensures that all the signals arrive simultaneously and allows listeners to switch stations without experiencing delays.

GPS also helps companies that operate in different parts of the world synchronize their computer networks and business transactions. Everything from stock trades and currency exchanges to credit card processing and online banking depend on the accurate time stamp provided by GPS satellite signals. In this way, the technology has become essential to the conduct of business and commerce worldwide.

GPS-based time synchronization also plays an important role in power transmission and distribution. Power plants and substations are equipped with GPS devices that time the flow of electricity through the power grid. Such precise timing enables engineers to trace the source of electrical anomalies and pinpoint the location of potential problems. GPS thus contributes to more efficient power distribution and fewer blackouts.

Improving Science and Agriculture

The impact of GPS technology also extends to science, agriculture, and the environment. Satellite tracking and imaging enables geographic information systems professionals to create detailed maps of the entire world. These maps can be adjusted digitally to emphasize various features and serve different purposes. They can be used for scientific research, environmental studies, agricultural planning, and a vast array of other applications.

Weather stations rely on GPS to monitor atmospheric changes, which help in forecasting weather and dangerous storms.

GPS satellite data has improved the accuracy of weather forecasting as well as the reporting of hazardous weather conditions to ships and planes. In 2009 researchers from the National Oceanic and Atmospheric Administration (NOAA) installed GPS weather stations on two offshore oil platforms in the Gulf of Mexico owned by Devon Energy. Through precise timing of the radio signals from GPS satellites, these weather stations enable climate scientists to measure the amount of moisture in the atmosphere. "The energy contained in a hurricane is related to the amount of moisture in the storm," says NOAA scientist Seth I. Gutman. "It's the exchange of moisture in the open ocean, and the exchange of moisture between the oceans and the atmosphere that determines whether or not there is the energy to sustain a storm, to intensify it, to reduce it."[9] Such applications of GPS technology could save lives and reduce property damage by enabling scientists to predict the path and intensity of storms, as well as the amount of rainfall and storm surge they will produce.

Scientists have also used GPS timing devices to monitor seismic activity (movements in the earth) and better anticipate earthquakes. These scientific applications of GPS technology can help save lives and reduce property damage. Scientists have also used GPS technology for a wide variety of other purposes, such as biological field studies, wildlife tracking, and climate change research. GPS makes data collection faster and easier, contributing to more accurate and valuable scientific research.

GPS technology is also vital to modern precision farming techniques. GPS satellites are used to collect data on the electromagnetic radiation reflected from farmland. "The spectrum of this radiation—which can be in the form of either natural sunlight or artificial radar—can reveal, with surprising precision, the properties of the soil, the quantity of crop being grown, and the levels in those crops of chlorophyll, various minerals, moisture and other indicators of their quality," notes a writer for *Economist* magazine. "If recent and forecast weather data are added to the mix, detailed maps can be produced indicating exactly how, where and when crops should be grown."[10] Cheaper and faster than sending soil samples to a laboratory for analysis, this technology enables farmers to increase the productivity of their land by up to 10 percent. An initiative that got underway in 2009 aimed to create digital soil maps of Africa in order to improve agricultural productivity in cultivated areas and locate new productive areas for farming. In this way, GPS has the potential to help combat world hunger.

Expanding Recreational Opportunities

GPS technology has expanded the realm of outdoor recreation to include entirely new activities, like geocaching, geodashing, and geotours. It has also introduced an added measure of safety and enjoyment to many conventional outdoor activities. Before the advent of handheld GPS receivers, explorers of the outdoors always risked becoming lost in unfamiliar terrain. They had to worry about their ability to navigate in darkness or in bad weather conditions. They had to ensure that their maps were up-to-date, that their compasses worked correctly, and that they paid close attention to trail markers and landmarks.

Although it is still a good idea to take these sensible precautions, GPS gives explorers much greater confidence in the outdoors. Hikers, bikers, snowmobilers, hunters, fishermen, and other outdoor enthusiasts who carry a GPS unit have the advantage of always knowing their current position and the route they followed to reach it. This information enables them to navigate safely in unfamiliar terrain and return to their starting point even if visibility becomes restricted. Outdoor enthusiasts can also transfer route information and waypoints to a computer in order to share their adventures with other people. This capability of GPS helps create communities of like-minded individuals and expands recreational opportunities for all.

Solar flares can interfere with GPS satellite signals. Flares are expected to increase at times, which could endanger vehicles relying on accurate navigational information.

Problems and Limitations

As GPS technology has expanded its reach, users have demanded and received ever-greater accuracy, integrity, and availability from the system. Yet the technology does have some significant limitations that users must keep in mind.

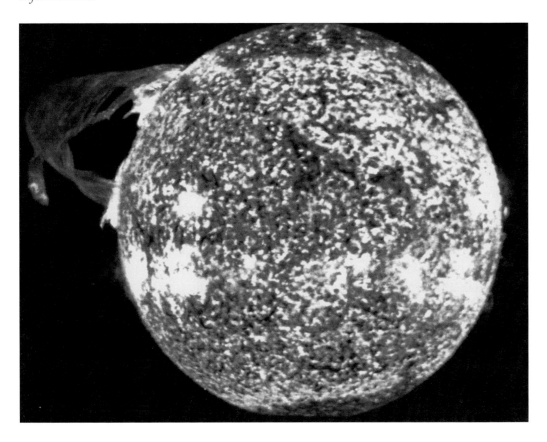

Satellite Geometry

The most accurate GPS positioning depends on good satellite geometry. In an ideal situation, GPS satellites are widely spaced in the sky above a user's position. When the visible satellites are closely grouped within the user's line of sight, the GPS receiver cannot calculate its position as accurately. The degree to which poor satellite geometry affects positioning performance is known as dilution of precision.

It is important not to become overly dependent upon GPS, just in case there is a problem with a receiver or a disruption of the satellite signal.

A number of atmospheric conditions can affect the integrity of GPS satellite signals. Ionospheric interference affects radio signals as they travel through the uppermost part of the earth's atmosphere, called the ionosphere. The ionosphere is made up of particles that receive an electrical charge from the sun's radiation. When a radio wave reaches the ionosphere, its electromagnetic energy causes the charged particles to move or oscillate in the same frequency. This property of the ionosphere serves to propagate or "bounce" the radio signal down to Earth. But the number of charged particles available to perform this function varies depending on the amount of radiation the ionosphere receives from the sun. As a result, satellite signals are delayed slightly as they pass through the ionosphere, but the amount of the delay depends on the time of day and season of the year at the point on Earth where the signals are received. To enable GPS receivers to correct for this delay, the satellites broadcast signals on two different frequencies. Ground-based navigation stations using DGPS or the Wide Area Augmentation System (WAAS) also send out correction information.

Solar flares are another source of atmospheric interference that can affect GPS satellite signals. As the sun burns, it occasionally releases bursts of electrically charged particles. These solar flares generate radio waves in the 1.2 and 1.6 gigahertz frequency bands used by GPS signals. GPS technology was originally developed at a time when solar activity was relatively low. But some experts claim that a predicted increase in solar flares in 2011 could cause significant disruptions to GPS signals. They are worried that this problem could cause potentially dangerous navigational errors for boats, planes, and emergency personnel if GPS satellites and receivers are not redesigned to compensate for the solar activity.

Obstacles on the ground can also interfere with the radio signals transmitted by GPS satellites. In order to determine its position accurately, a GPS receiver needs to get signals from at least four satellites. Because the precise timing of the signals is so important, they must travel in a straight line and reach the receiver directly. If the signals bounce off of tall objects on Earth, such as buildings or rock walls, the travel time increases and navigational errors can occur. This common problem is called a multipath error. GPS receivers must have a clear view of the sky in order to lock on to satellite signals, so they will not operate correctly indoors, underwater, or in dense forests, narrow valleys, deep canyons, or caves. "It is impossible to predict when the terrain will limit GPS reception," writes Lawrence Letham in his book *GPS Made Easy*. "You cannot tell from a map if an area will block the satellite signals, because you do not know the satellites' positions relative to the terrain."[11]

GPS satellites are also subject to a number of other problems that can affect the quality of the signals they transmit. Ephemeris errors occur when the almanac of orbital information is out of date, causing satellites to report their positions inaccurately. Some remote locations on Earth suffer from poor satellite geometry, meaning that the visible satellites tend to "line up" from the perspective of the GPS user, rather than assuming the widely spaced configuration that is best for trilateration. Since the orbital positions of GPS satellites are arranged in a pattern that offers good geometry to users in heavily populated areas, the satellites visible to users in remote locations—like northern Alaska—may appear to be grouped together at a low angle along the horizon. Poor satellite geometry causes these users to experience a high dilution of precision (DOP) in the signals they receive.

Finally, GPS receivers can and do fail for a variety of reasons. Like other electronic devices, they can be sensitive to moisture and to extremely high or low temperatures. They also operate on batteries, which can lose their charge unexpectedly. "Never stake your life on a pair of AA batteries!"[12] writes Donald Cooke in his book *Fun with GPS*. The maps available for GPS units sometimes contain errors, and they become outdated quickly. In addition GPS users must always face the possibility that they could damage or lose their receiver.

Given all of these potential problems and limitations, it is vital that GPS users view the technology as an aid to navigation, rather than as a substitute for basic map-reading skills and common sense. This is especially true when people engage in outdoor pursuits that take them far away from sources of help. "GPS receivers are marvelous devices," write Bob Burns and Mike Burns in their book *Wilderness Navigation*. "Keep in mind, however, that they are not absolutely foolproof, and that topography, forest cover, battery life, electronic failure, and cold temperatures can cause problems in their use. A GPS receiver cannot replace conventional map and compass techniques."[13]

Modernizing GPS Technology

The growing importance of GPS technology in modern life has led to a number of efforts to compensate for errors and ensure that the system performs accurately and reliably. For instance, the U.S. government has developed several different augmentation systems that work in conjunction with GPS. The Nationwide Differential GPS (NDGPS) is a network of ground-based radio towers that extends across the United States. NDGPS-equipped receivers can use the ground signals from known locations to check the accuracy of satellite-based signals. The Wide Area Augmentation System (WAAS), operated by the Federal Aviation Administration (FAA), uses stationary satellites to transmit navigational signals to aircraft. WAAS makes GPS satellite signals accurate and reliable enough to be used as the primary navigation system onboard certain types of aircraft.

In addition to augmenting the existing GPS signals to increase their accuracy, the U.S. government is committed to a continuous program of modernizing GPS technology. One part of this program involves replacing and upgrading the constellation of GPS satellites in space. The original eleven GPS satellites were designated as Block I, and they were mostly used for testing and development purposes. Beginning in 1987 the Block I satellites were replaced by twenty-six Block II and IIA (augmentation) satellites, which had a longer useful life.

In 1997 the first Block IIR (replenishment) satellites were launched. These advanced satellites were equipped with reprogrammable processors that enabled ground-monitoring stations to fix problems and make adjustments while the satellites were in orbit. Beginning in 2005, Block IIR satellites were modified to transmit a stronger and more accurate civil signal. The next-generation Block IIF satellites—which promised increased accuracy, improved reliability, more power, and a third civil signal—were originally scheduled to begin replacing older models in 2008. A series of technical problems and cost overruns caused the first launch to be delayed until May 2010. "The new GPS IIF satellites bring key improvements, including a more jam-resistant military signal, a new civil signal to enhance commercial aviation and search-and-rescue operations, and significantly improved signal accuracy as more of these new satellites go into operation,"[14] says Craig Cooning of Boeing, the aerospace company that developed the technology.

The satellites of the future are designated as GPS Block III. Scheduled to begin launching in 2014, they are expected to vastly expand the capabilities of the current system. For instance, GPS III satellites will enable U.S. military leaders to shut off navigation signals to certain geographical areas in order to prevent enemy forces from using the system. GPS III satellites will also feature five hundred times greater signal power to make them more resistant to jamming. In addition, the new technology will be fully

A Dual Role for GPS Satellites

GPS was originally developed for military use, and it has continued to serve military functions throughout its history. For instance, modern GPS satellites are equipped with monitoring sensors designed to detect nuclear weapon explosions and assess strike damage. This application of satellite technology grew out of the 1963 Limited Nuclear Test Ban Treaty and 1968 Nuclear Non-Proliferation Treaty signed by the United States and the Soviet Union. These treaties prohibited nuclear testing on land, underwater, or in space. At first the U.S. military developed special satellites for the purpose of ensuring compliance. Beginning in the 1980s, NAVSTAR and GPS satellites were also equipped with sensors to expand the military's nuclear monitoring capability.

compatible with global navigation systems under development in Europe, Russia, and elsewhere.

The GPS III program was developed in recognition of how valuable GPS technology has become to both military and civilian users. Its objective is to meet their constantly evolving needs by providing the greatest possible accuracy, reliability, and security. GPS III is expected to resolve some of the problems and limitations in the current GPS system, thus reducing the potential for serious disruptions to transportation, public safety, military operations, and economic activities in the future.

CHAPTER **5**

Future Uses and Advancements of the Global Positioning System

In less than two decades, the Global Positioning System (GPS) has gone from a space-age military technology to a public utility used by millions of people as part of their daily routines. Average Americans only became aware of the satellite-based navigation system after U.S. forces demonstrated its amazing capabilities during the Persian Gulf War. Civilians did not even have access to the full benefits of GPS until 2000, when the U.S. government made the most accurate positional data available to all users. By 2010, however, GPS-enabled navigation and tracking devices could be found virtually anywhere—in cars, airplanes, boats, delivery trucks, shipping containers, emergency vehicles, farm tractors, construction equipment, scientific research stations, telecommunications networks, electrical power grids, and even pet collars. Most remarkable of all, nearly 60 million people carried the technology around with them in their pockets, purses, or backpacks in the form of a GPS-equipped smartphone, according to a 2009 study conducted by the technology research firm iSuppli.

EXISTING GLOBAL NAVIGATION SATELLITE SYSTEMS (GNSS)

As of July 2010, there were 4 global navigation satellite systems in existence, or in some stage of development. There are also several regional navigation satellite systems in operation, development, or planning stages, which are meant to augment, or add to, the GNSS. These include: IRNSS (India), QZSS (Japan), NigComSat (Nigeria), BeiDou (China), WAAS (U.S.), SDCM (Russia), and EGNOS (E.U.).

Country	Name	Status	# of Expected Satellites
U.S.A.	GPS (NAVSTAR)	Operational	32
Russia	GLONASS (Global Navigation Satellite System)	Operational	24
European Union (E.U.)	Galileo	In development	30
China	Compass	In development	30

Taken from http://en.rian.ru/infographics/20100610/159371756.html

Since GPS technology is developing so rapidly—and new consumer GPS devices and applications appear every day—the potential for future advances seems almost unlimited. "With GPS, the world has been given a technology of unbounded promise,"[15] note scientist Daniel Kleppner and science journalist Gary Taubes, writing for the National Academy of Sciences. At the same time, though, the relentlessly fast-paced march of GPS technology has raised concerns about society's ability to keep up. For instance, some people question what will happen to personal privacy in a world where portable GPS units make it possible to track an individual's location

GLONASS vs. GPS

There are currently only two GNSS that are considered fully operational: the Russian GLONASS and the American GPS. The two systems have different satellite configurations, with GLONASS using 3 orbital planes, and GPS using 6. As of July 2010, GPS had 30 satellites orbiting at full capacity and an additional 2 in commission, while GLONASS had 21 at full capacity and 2 spare satellites in orbit.

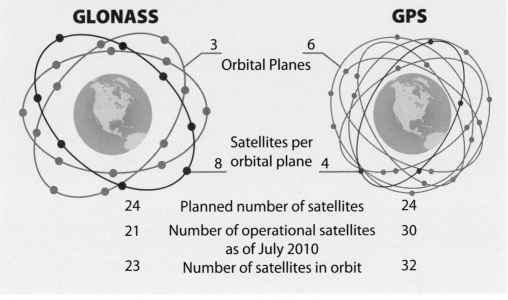

GLONASS		GPS
3	Orbital Planes	6
8	Satellites per orbital plane	4
24	Planned number of satellites	24
21	Number of operational satellites as of July 2010	30
23	Number of satellites in orbit	32

Taken from http://en.rian.ru/infographics/20100610/159371756.html

at all times. Others wonder whether spontaneity and a sense of adventure will cease to exist in an age when portable GPS units can be carried into even the most remote wilderness areas. Finally, some critics worry that GPS has assumed such a vital role in modern life that there is a potential for a global catastrophe if GPS technology suddenly were to fail.

Navigational Advances for Transportation

The transportation sector is expected to be the focus of many exciting future developments in GPS technology. "One can imagine a 21st century world covered by

an augmented GPS and laced with mobile digital communications in which aircraft and other vehicles travel through 'virtual tunnels,' imaginary tracks through space which are continuously optimized for weather, traffic, and other conditions," says Bradford W. Parkinson, one of the people responsible for developing GPS. "Robotic vehicles perform all sorts of construction, transportation, mining, and earth-moving functions working day and night with no need to rest."[16]

With ever-increasing numbers of automobiles equipped with GPS navigation capability, many people envision GPS-based road-traffic management systems being developed in the future. New cars could be equipped with sophisticated GPS devices deeply integrated into the vehicle's electrical and communication systems. This device, which would be similar to the black boxes carried by commercial airplanes, would record data about the vehicle's location, direction, and speed, as well as the driver's use of brakes, turn signals, or seat belts. It could also communicate that data to traffic-management stations that monitor road conditions and traffic flow within limited geographic areas. Whenever a certain number of cars reported a decrease in speed or an increase in braking, the system could alert nearby drivers about a potential traffic jam and suggest alternative routes.

This sort of traffic-management system could also be connected with existing systems, like OnStar, which sense when a vehicle has been in an accident and automatically notifies emergency personnel. The exact location of all accidents could be automatically reported to traffic-management systems and passed along to other drivers, along with instructions on how to avoid the area. This capability would help prevent further accidents and enable emergency personnel to respond more quickly.

A common concern about the use of GPS navigation equipment in moving vehicles is the potential for distracted drivers to become involved in accidents. To address this problem, future automotive GPS units could feature an innovative display that projects a three-dimensional image onto the car's windshield. The image would appear as if it were suspended over the road, enabling the driver to see any approaching obstacles at the same time as they consult GPS route-planning information. This sort of in-car display could be integrated with a variety of GPS-enabled devices, including cellular phones, laptop computers, and handheld units. Some people believe that in the distant future GPS navigation might enable cars to operate with very limited input from drivers. Under these scenarios, specially equipped vehicles could use GPS technology to drive themselves on preprogrammed routes.

Next-Generation Air-Traffic Control Systems

GPS technology also holds a great deal of promise for increasing the safety and efficiency of the nation's air-traffic control system. The Federal Aviation Administration (FAA) is in the process of developing a sophisticated new method of guiding an aircraft that combines GPS satellite navigation with a Ground-Based Augmentation System (GBAS). The proposed GBAS project, known as NextGen, would replace aging, radar-based, air-traffic control systems that cost the FAA over $300 million annually to maintain. It would involve placing four differential GPS receivers at precisely surveyed locations near every airport in the United States. These receivers would provide stationary reference points to correct GPS satellite signals and broadcast correction information to incoming aircraft within a 30-mile (48km) radius.

When fully implemented, NextGen could increase the accuracy of GPS navigational data to within 3 feet (1m) both vertically and laterally. This degree of precision has the potential to triple airspace capacity, improve safety, reduce delays, and save fuel. "NextGen would help airliners fly, land, and takeoff closer together, minimizing delays," writes Michael Tarm in America's Intelligence Wire. "Even though the technology would allow more planes into the sky, the FAA and pilots agree that the technology would actually reduce the risk of accidents such as midair collisions and runway incursions."[17]

Proponents of NextGen point out that existing air-traffic control systems force commercial airplanes to fly long, zigzagging routes between ground towers, costing U.S. airlines billions of dollars annually in wasted fuel. They claim that the route efficiencies possible with NextGen could save $5 billion in fuel per year. Although the FAA budget did not cover the estimated $35 billion cost of implementation as of early 2010, airline industry insiders expect the switch to NextGen to take place by 2020.

GPS-Enabled Smartphones Take Over

Another development expected to have a significant impact on the future uses of GPS technology is the rapidly increasing popularity of smartphones. These devices not only feature an integrated GPS receiver, but they also have the ability to connect to the Internet for instant access to online maps, addresses, and other navigational aids. Most smartphones

can provide turn-by-turn directions—either by displaying them on a screen or by voice through the phone's speaker—and many models can also work as a tracking device. In the future, more smartphones will be programmed with location-based service (LBS) applications that automatically deliver news, traffic, weather, coupons, advertisements, and other information to users based on their location.

Technical issues hindered the adoption of GPS into smartphones in the mid-2000s. Early GPS-enabled phones had a number of shortcomings, including small display screens, difficult-to-use interfaces, and limited memory and battery power. Many units had trouble receiving satellite signals while indoors or suffered connection interruptions whenever the user had an incoming call. In addition, many service providers charged high monthly fees for use of GPS navigation capabilities. By 2010, however, major smartphone brands like Blackberry, Palm, and iPhone had overcome most of these problems. Newer models featured improved screens and interfaces, more memory and battery power, and a variety of maps and navigational applications.

Smartphones like the Motorola Droid use GPS technology to automatically provide information users, including news, weather, and directions.

As a result of these improvements, industry analysts view smartphones as the GPS receivers of the future. "The smartphone is beginning to displace yet another stand-alone device—the GPS receiver—as a convenient way for drivers to get directions to unknown destinations,"[18] writes Jenna Wortham in the *New York Times*. Sales of traditional, handheld GPS receivers by such manufacturers as Garmin, TomTom, and Magellan slowed considerably in 2009 as shipments of GPS-enabled smartphones grew, and this trend was predicted to accelerate in the future. According to an iSuppli study, sales of standalone portable navigation devices were expected to show modest growth, from 114 million units in 2009 to 130 million units in 2011, before leveling off in 2014. In the meantime, sales of GPS-enabled smartphones were expected to more than double from 58 million in 2009 to 117 million in 2011, and then more than double again to exceed 300 million by 2014. The huge market for smartphones demonstrates the exploding popularity of GPS technology as a part of everyday life.

Tracking Property, People, and Pets

GPS technology is also expected to expand beyond smartphones and become incorporated into a wide range of other mobile electronic devices, from laptop computers, gaming consoles, and media players to watches, digital cameras, and pet collars. Scientists and engineers face a number of technical issues in ensuring the seamless integration of these technologies. "With GPS well on the way to becoming a ubiquitous [common] feature across the mobile consumer space, GPS chipsets are subject to increasingly challenging requirements," says analyst Dominique Bonte of ABI Research. "Many new LBS services such as social networking, tracking, logging, and geo-tagging require always-on, instant operation even in the absence of network assistance and without sacrificing battery life or increasing cost."[19]

One of the main benefits of incorporating GPS technology into mobile devices is the ability to track and locate lost or stolen property. The tracking capability offered by GPS can also be used to locate lost people and pets. For example, parents can attach a GPS-enabled device to a child's clothing or backpack and receive notification if the child strays outside of a designated safe zone. The same type of device can be attached to pet collars to help locate missing animals. Doctors with the U.S. Centers for Disease Control and Prevention have even launched a program to track the movements of asthma sufferers in certain cities or geographic regions. By comparing the routes traveled by different people with real-time data about their symptoms, doctors hope to map sources of pollution that contribute to asthma attacks and direct sufferers away from those areas. They believe that GPS technology can help their patients control their symptoms and achieve a better quality of life.

GPS technology allows scientists to track endangered wildlife such as the puffin and monitor their numbers. It can also be used to track pets.

Privacy and Other Concerns

Although the tracking capability of GPS-enabled mobile devices has a number of valuable applications, it also raises concerns about privacy. Some businesses make use of the tracking function to monitor their employees. While tracking delivery or service vehicles seems like a legitimate use of GPS, some critics argue that routinely using the technology to check up on the location of employees when they leave the office strays into the realm of invasion of privacy. There are also questions surrounding the use of GPS tracking by rental car companies. In-car GPS devices can provide rental companies with detailed information about where a customer drove and whether they exceeded the speed limit. While this type of information could legitimately help the company set fair rental rates, it could also make customers feel uncomfortable if it was used without their knowledge or consent.

The tracking capability of GPS technology has a number of interesting applications in law enforcement. GPS experts predict a future in which police will be able to place GPS tracking devices on a suspect's car in order to follow them remotely and monitor their activity. They could also use the technology to follow former criminals who are released from prison on probation or people who have been served with restraining orders.

This GPS application has already been introduced on a limited basis. Several states require convicted sex offenders, stalkers, or domestic abusers to wear GPS monitoring devices. These devices alert police if the offenders enter a geographic exclusion zone near their victims' home, school, or workplace. If the offender tries to remove the electronic tracking device, they violate their probation and can be put in prison. Proponents of this practice claim that GPS technology plays an important role in protecting potential victims. "Using GPS monitoring to enforce an order of protection makes the order more than just a piece of paper," says Diane Rosenfeld, a lecturer at Harvard Law School. "It's a way of making the criminal justice system treat domestic violence as potentially serious. By detecting any escalation in the behavior of a batterer, GPS can prevent unnecessary tragedies."[20] Opponents, on the other hand, argue that continued GPS tracking of men and women who have completed their prison terms represents cruel and unusual punishment.

Like many new technologies, GPS tracking has developed faster than legislation to regulate its use. In the absence of state and federal laws on the subject, it has fallen to the courts to decide how and when law enforcement officials can legally use GPS tracking without violating people's civil rights. One of the most contentious issues involves whether police need a warrant—a judge's order allowing law enforcement officers to carry out certain activities, such as searches, wiretapping, or arrests—to place GPS tracking devices on suspects' vehicles. In May 2009 an appeals court in Wisconsin ruled

Detecting RFI and Preventing Signal Jamming

GPS satellite signals are very weak compared to other types of radio signals. Regular cell phone signals, for instance, are billions of times stronger. Under favorable conditions, GPS receivers do a good job of picking out the satellite signals from the background noise of other radio signals. But GPS signals are still subject to interference from physical obstacles, like tall buildings or trees, or from radio frequency interference (RFI) by other transmitters operating on similar frequencies. When RFI is strong enough, it can jam the receiver, preventing it from picking up any satellite signals. Intentional jamming by hostile forces is a concern for military users of GPS, while civilian users can sometimes fall victim to unintentional jamming. In 2007, for example, an inadvertent jamming incident occurred in the harbor in San Diego, California, that caused all GPS receivers within a 9-mile (14.4km) radius to fail. Scientists and engineers are working to improve GPS receivers so that they can detect RFI and be more resistant to jamming.

European GPS Systems

Although the American Global Positioning System (GPS) is the best-known satellite navigation system in the world, several other countries operate their own equivalent systems. The Russian Global Orbiting Navigation Satellite System (GLONASS) launched its first satellite in 1983 and became fully operational in 1995. All of the ground-control stations are located within the Russian Federation, but the system can be used anywhere in the world. As of 2010, GLONASS featured twenty-one satellites and provided civilian users with 328-foot (100m) accuracy and military users with 33-foot (10m) accuracy.

The European Union decided to develop its own global satellite navigation system, Galileo, in the event that the United States and Russia chose to disable their systems for any reason. The Galileo project launched its first satellite in 2005 and was expected to become fully operational by 2014. With thirty satellites in orbit and ground-control centers in Germany and Italy, Galileo was predicted to more than double existing GPS coverage in the United States and provide more precise location information than was available previously. To use these European navigation systems in addition to American GPS, users will need specially equipped receivers that can interpret all available satellite signals, known as Global Navigation Satellite System receivers.

that warrantless tracking was allowable. The judges said that the use of GPS monitoring equipment did not violate the constitutional protection against unreasonable search and seizure because it was no more invasive than traditional police surveillance. But courts in other states have ruled that warrantless GPS tracking is only permissible while a vehicle is on public property, or that a warrant is required under all circumstances. "There will no doubt be many more federal and state court rulings about the constitutionality of warrantless GPS monitoring," notes an editorial in the *New York Times*. "It is never easy to fit modern technology into the broad privacy principles that the drafters of the federal and state constitutions laid out."[21]

Privacy is just one of many areas of concern that surround possible future uses of GPS technology. Some analysts worry that society has grown too dependent upon GPS.

If satellite navigation were ever disrupted or disabled—by a war, a terrorist attack, a solar flare, a technical malfunction, or even the reinstatement of Selective Availability by the U.S. government—it has the potential to cause a global catastrophe. Such an event could cripple the U.S. military and shut down major parts of the world's telecommunication systems, financial networks, and transportation services. "It is frightening to think the world depends so much on these complicated devices and their functioning correctly,"[22] writes Caleb Johnson in an article on the Web site Switched.

Some critics wonder if the ever-increasing reliance on GPS navigation will cause people to miss out on spontaneous adventures, the thrill of discovering new places, and the sense of accomplishment that comes from finding their own way. "What do we lose," writes David Amsden in *GQ* magazine, "if no one is ever lost? It's hard not to conjure up a future in which everyone will rely on some form of GPS to inform him of where he is and where he is going: a future, in other words, in which the possibility of being lost has been eradicated from human experience. Which, if you think about it, is kind of frightening."[23]

NOTES

Introduction: A Revolution in Navigation

1. Daniel Kleppner, adapted by Gary Taubes, "GPS: The Role of Atomic Clocks," National Academy of Sciences, April 1997, www.beyonddiscovery.org/content/view.page.asp?I=468.
2. Stephen T. Powers and Brad Parkinson, "The Origins of GPS, Part 1," *GPS World*, May 1, 2010, www.gpsworld.com/gnss-system/gps-modernization/the-origins-gps-part-1-9890.

Chapter 1: A Brief History of Navigation Systems

3. Quoted in Federal Aviation Administration, "Navigation Services," Federal Aviation Administration, May 1, 2000, www.faa.gov/about/office_org/headquarters_offices/ato/service_units/techops/navservices/gnss/gps/policy/presidential/index.cfm.

Chapter 3: Uses of Global Positioning System Technology

4. Andrew Marshall, "In Search of Ourselves," *Time International*, June 29, 2009, p. 87.
5. Scott Pace, et al., *The Global Positioning System: Assessing National Policies*, Santa Monica, CA: Rand, 1995, p. 245.
6. J.R. Wilson, "The Future of Precision-Guided Munitions," *Military & Aerospace Electronics*, December 20, 2009, p. 20.
7. Linda Williams, *Great Inventions: Navigational Aids*, New York: Marshall Cavendish, 2008, p. 109.

Chapter 4: Impact of Global Positioning System Technology

8. Jules McNeff, "GPS World: That Was Then," *GPS World*, January 2010, p. 8.
9. Quoted in Cain Burdeau, "Hurricane Researchers Hope GPS Will Help Predict Impact of Storms,"

Associated Press, March 16, 2010, http://blog.al.com/live/2010/03/hurricane_researchers_hope_gps.html.

10. *Economist*, "Harvest Moon: Artificial Satellites Are Helping Farmers Improve Crop Yields," *Economist*, November 5, 2009.

11. Lawrence Letham, *GPS Made Easy: Using Global Positioning Systems in the Outdoors*, Seattle, WA: Mountaineers, 1996, p. 6.

12. Donald Cooke, *Fun with GPS*, Redlands, CA: ESRI, 2005, p. 2.

13. Bob Burns and Mike Burns, *Wilderness Navigation: Finding Your Way Using Map, Compass, Altimeter, and GPS*, Seattle, WA: Mountaineers, 2004, p. 107.

14. Quoted in Europe Intelligence Wire, "Next-Generation GPS Satellite Launches Successfully," Europe Intelligence Wire, May 29, 2010.

Chapter 5: Future Uses and Advancements of the Global Positioning System

15. Kleppner, "GPS: The Role of Atomic Clocks and the Future."

16. Quoted in GPS.gov, "GPS Augmentations," GPS.gov, www.gps.gov/systems/augmentations.

17. Michael Tarm, "GPS Could Save Airlines Time and Fuel," America's Intelligence Wire, October 10, 2008.

18. Jenna Wortham, "Sending GPS Devices the Way of the Tape Deck?" *New York Times*, July 8, 2009.

19. Quoted in *Wireless News*, "ABI Research: GPS IC Shipments Will Approach 450 Million in 2010," *Wireless News*, October 2, 2009.

20. Quoted in Ariana Green, "More States Using GPS to Track Abusers and Stalkers," *New York Times*, May 9, 2009, http://www.nytimes.com/2009/05/09/us/09gps.html.

21. *New York Times*, "GPS and Privacy Rights," *New York Times*, May 15, 2009, http://www.nytimes.com/2009/11/23/opinion/23mon3.html?_r=1&scp=1&sq=gps%20and%20privacy%20rights&st=cse.

22. Caleb Johnson, "GPS Glitches Cause Concern over Future of Satellites," Switched, June 18, 2009, www.switched.com/2009/06/18/gps-glitches-cause-concern-over-future-of-satellites.

23. David Amsden, "The Lost Art of Getting Lost," *GQ*, July 2009, p. 46.

atomic clock: An extremely precise timekeeping device used on GPS satellites. It operates by measuring the magnetic resonance frequency of atoms.

coordinate: A geographical position expressed in degrees of latitude and longitude.

Differential GPS (DGPS): A network of ground-based radio antennas that calculates the degree of inaccuracy in satellite signals and provides correction information to GPS receivers.

geocaching: A high-tech treasure hunt game in which participants use GPS receivers to search for hidden objects at specific coordinates.

GPS monitoring station: A control center on the ground that tracks GPS satellites and communicates with them as needed to adjust their orbits, synchronize their atomic clocks, and update their navigational information.

GPS receiver: An electronic device that interprets radio signals from GPS satellites and uses the information to calculate a position.

GPS satellite: A manmade spacecraft that orbits Earth and transmits radio signals that can be used in navigation.

latitude: A measure of location in degrees north or south of the equator.

longitude: A measure of location in degrees east or west of the prime meridian.

navigation: The practice of guiding or directing a means of transport by determining its position, direction, and distance traveled.

Selective Availability (SA): A program instituted by the U.S. government that intentionally degraded the quality of GPS navigational signals available to nonmilitary users until 2000.

trilateration: A mathematical method of using the known locations of at least three objects to figure out the unknown location of another object.

waypoint: Coordinates for a destination that can be stored in the memory of a GPS receiver.

FOR MORE INFORMATION

Books

Ahmed Al-Rabbany, *Introduction to GPS: The Global Positioning System*. Norwood, MA: Artech House, 2006. Informative for students and professionals alike, this book provides an overview of GPS technology as well as details on satellite positioning, signal errors and corrections, and future applications.

Lawrence Harte and Ben Levitan, *GPS Quick Course: Technology, Systems, and Operation*. Fuquay Varina, NC: Althos, 2007. This book offers a clear, concise explanation of each segment of GPS technology as well as a survey of its applications and impact.

Lawrence Letham, *GPS Made Easy: Using Global Positioning Systems in the Outdoors*, 5th ed. Seattle WA: Mountaineers, 2008. This guidebook provides a solid overview of the usefulness and limitations of GPS in outdoor navigation and recreation.

Jeanne Sturm, *GPS: Global Positioning System*. Vero Beach, FL: Rourke, 2009. This concise, understandable book for young readers outlines the basic technology and major uses of GPS.

Linda Williams, *Great Inventions: Navigational Aids*. New York: Marshall Cavendish, 2008. This readable history of human navigation concludes with a chapter on GPS.

Internet Sources

Peter H. Dana, "Global Positioning System Overview," University of Colorado at Boulder Geography Department (Web site), 1999, www.colorado.edu/geography/gcraft/notes/gps/gps_f.html.

Stephen T. Powers and Bradford Parkinson, "The Origins of GPS," *GPS World*, May 1, 2010 and June 1, 2010, www.gpsworld.com/gnss-system/gps-modernization/the-origins-gps-part-1-9890.

Periodical

Andrew Marshall, "In Search of Ourselves," *Time International*, June 29, 2009.

Web Sites

Federal Aviation Administration (www.faa.gov). This site provides a clear overview of how GPS works, along with answers to frequently asked questions, and links to other resources. Select "A to Z Index" on the home page and then look for "Global Positioning System."

Global Positioning System (www.gps .gov). This U.S. government site is dedicated to explaining GPS technology, its applications, and its impact on modern society.

Smithsonian National Air and Space Museum (www.nasm.si.edu). This site offers GPS: A New Constellation, an online exhibit that provides the historical development, technical workings, and applications of GPS technology.

Trimble (www.trimble.com). This corporate Web site offers a GPS tutorial that explains GPS technology, how it works, and how it is used.

INDEX

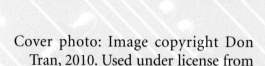

PICTURE CREDITS

Cover photo: Image copyright Don Tran, 2010. Used under license from Shutterstock.com

© adam eastland/Alamy, 39

© Andrea Rescigno/Alamy, 34

AP Images, 16, 43, 51, 58, 60, 64, 66, 76, 79, 81

© Bettmann/Corbis, 28

© Charles W Luzier/Reuters/Corbis, 23

© Chris Howes/Wild Places Photography/Alamy, 8

© Durand-Hudson-Langevin-Orban/Sygma/Corbis, 9

© Eddie Gerald/Alamy, 13

© Friedrich Saurer/Alamy, 8

Gale, a part of Cengage Learning, 14, 31, 37, 56, 74, 75

Image copyright kaczor58, 2010. Used under license from Shutterstock .com, 35

Image copyright Zlatko Guzmic, 2010. Used under license from Shutterstock.com, 15

© imagebroker/Alamy, 21

© Markus Altmann/Corbis, 70

© Michael Venture/Alamy, 9

© Peter Casolino/Alamy, 9

© Roger Bamber/Alamy, 45

© Roger Ressmeyer/Corbis, 49

© William Whitehurst/Corbis, 27

© William Taufic/Corbis, 29

ABOUT THE AUTHOR

Laurie Collier Hillstrom is a freelance writer and editor. She is the author of more than twenty books, including *Technology 360: Online Social Networks*, *Defining Moments: The Attack on Pearl Harbor*, and *People in the News: Al Gore*. She lives in Michigan with her husband, Kevin, and twin daughters, Allison and Lindsay.